*Culture and
Customs of
Egypt*

**Recent Titles in
Culture and Customs of Africa**

Culture and Customs of Egypt

Molefi Kete Asante

Culture and Customs of Africa
Toyin Falola, Series Editor

GREENWOOD PRESS
Westport, Connecticut • London

Library of Congress Cataloging-in-Publication Data

Asante, Molefi K., 1942–
  Culture and customs of Egypt / Molefi Kete Asante.
      p. cm.—(Culture and customs of Africa, ISSN 1530–8367)
    Includes bibliographical references and index.
    ISBN 0–313–31740–2 (alk. paper)
    1. Egypt—Social life and customs. I. Title. II. Series.
  DT70.A83   2002
  962—dc21   2002021620

British Library Cataloguing in Publication Data is available.

Library of Congress Catalog Card Number: 2002021620
ISBN: 0–313–31740–2
ISSN: 1530–8367

First published in 2002

Greenwood Press, 88 Post Road West, Westport, CT 06881
An imprint of Greenwood Publishing Group, Inc.
www.greenwood.com

Printed in the United States of America

The paper used in this book complies with the
Permanent Paper Standard issued by the National
Information Standards Organization (Z39.48–1984).

10 9 8 7 6 5 4

Contents

Series Foreword

AFRICA is a vast continent, the second largest, after Asia. It is four times the size of the United States, excluding Alaska. It is the cradle of human civilization. A diverse continent, Africa has more than fifty countries with a population of over 700 million people who speak over 1,000 languages. Ecological and cultural differences vary from one region to another. As an old continent, Africa is one of the richest in culture and customs, and its contributions to world civilization are impressive indeed.

Africans regard culture as essential to their lives and future development. Culture embodies their philosophy, worldview, behavior patterns, arts, and institutions. The books in this series intend to capture the comprehensiveness of African culture and customs, dwelling on such important aspects as religion, worldview, literature, media, art, housing, architecture, cuisine, traditional dress, gender, marriage, family, lifestyles, social customs, music, and dance.

The uses and definitions of "culture" vary, reflecting its prestigious association with civilization and social status, its restriction to attitude and behavior, its globalization, and the debates surrounding issues of tradition, modernity, and postmodernity. The participating authors have chosen a comprehensive meaning of culture while not ignoring the alternative uses of the term.

Each volume in the series focuses on a single country, and the format is uniform. The first chapter presents a historical overview, in addition to information on geography, economy, and politics. Each volume then proceeds to examine the various aspects of culture and customs. The series highlights the mechanisms for the transmission of tradition and culture across generations: the significance of orality, traditions, kinship rites, and family property distribution; the rise of print culture; and the impact of educational institutions. The series also explores the intersections between local, regional, national, and global bases for identity and social relations. While the volumes are organized nationally, they pay attention to ethnicity and language groups and the links between Africa and the wider world.

The books in the series capture the elements of continuity and change in culture and customs. Custom is not represented as static or as a museum artifact, but as a dynamic phenomenon. Furthermore, the authors recognize the current challenges to traditional wisdom, which include gender relations; the negotiation of local identities in relation to the state; the significance of struggles for power at national and local levels and their impact on cultural traditions and community-based forms of authority; and the tensions between agrarian and industrial/manufacturing/oil-based economic modes of production.

Africa is a continent of great changes, instigated mainly by Africans but also through influences from other continents. The rise of youth culture, the penetration of the global media, and the challenges to generational stability are some of the components of modern changes explored in the series. The ways in which traditional (non-Western and nonimitative) African cultural forms continue to survive and thrive, that is, how they have taken advantage of the market system to enhance their influence and reproduction also receive attention.

Through the books in this series, readers can see their own cultures in a different perspective, understand the habits of Africans, and educate themselves about the customs and cultures of other countries and people. The hope is that the readers will come to respect the cultures of others and see them not as inferior or superior to theirs, but merely as different. Africa has always been important to Europe and the United States, essentially as a source of labor, raw materials, and markets. Blacks are in Europe and the Americas as part of the African diaspora, a migration that took place primarily due to the slave trade. Recent African migrants increasingly swell their number and visibility. It is important to understand the history of the diaspora and the newer migrants, as well as the roots of the culture and customs of the places from where they come. It is equally important to understand others in order to be able to interact successfully in a world that keeps shrinking. The accessible nature of the books in this series will contribute to this understanding and enhance the quality of human interaction in a new millennium.

Toyin Falola
Frances Higginbothom Nalle Centennial Professor of History
The University of Texas at Austin

Preface

EGYPT is unequaled for its long history, monuments, and antiquities. Its wonders have attracted visitors for many centuries and its irresistible sources of wisdom and knowledge have inspired hundreds of thousands of ancient and contemporary students. When Herodotus, the Greek historian, wrote in 450 B.C. about the incredible sights and revelations of the land that was ancient even when he saw it, his treatise became famous as one of the first histories in the world.

To write a book on modern Egypt means that one is always writing with the thought of ancient Egypt in the background; so vast is the tapestry of its rich history that almost every instance of the present history is affected by the previous experiences on the land. Yet modern Egypt is not the same as ancient Egypt. Much like the face of modern America, Egypt has changed in the composition of its people, the religion of its people, and many of the cultural artifacts of the land. However, underneath the facade of changes that one can observe are attitudes and behaviors that hark back to the days of the pharaohs.

My objective in this book is to provide the reader with an accessible portrait of the contemporary nation of Egypt. Its history through the ages has been written and rewritten by many commentators, scholars, and students. The land the Arabs gave the name "Misr" was called by the Greeks "Egypt"— that is, "Aguptos"—but was referred to by the ancient Africans as "Kemet," the Black Country. They referred to it as the "gift of the Nile" and as the "Two Lands": Upper Egypt and Lower Egypt. Sometimes they called it "Ta Meri" meaning the "beloved land." Today the country is the most populous nation in the Arab cultural sphere although it is located on the African continent. It is the second most populous nation of Africa, after Nigeria. As a nation at the crossroads, Egypt is a cosmopolitan society with many cultural currents in its modern social and political structure. While this is true, Arabic culture is the dominant presence in the modern era.

Chronology

639–641 C.E.   Arab armies arrived in Egypt from Arabia and Syria at the request of Egyptians who sought their support in ousting the Romans. General El As's forces helped to throw off the Romans but quickly consolidated his hold on the country.

658–750   Ummayad Period when the ruling Islamic class was authorized from Damascus, Syria.

750–868   Abbasid Period when the ruling Islamic class was directed from Baghdad. The Abbasids claimed descent from Abbas, the uncle of the Prophet Muhammad.

868–905   Tulunid Period produced two major figures, Ahmad Tulun and Khumarayh Ahmad, whose authority stretched from Cairo to Cilicia.

905–935   Abbasids, Second Period, the reassertion of the Baghdad rule and the expansion of Islam.

935–969   Ikshids came to power and controlled both Egypt and Syria.

969–1171   Fatimid leaders traced their ancestry to Fatimah, the daughter of the Prophet Muhammad, and embraced the Shi'a doctrine.

1171–1250   Ayyubid Period, which was dominated by Salah ad-Din who reigned for twenty-four years. He spent eight years of his reign in Cairo during which time he established schools, built hospitals, and improved the infrastructure of the city. He introduced slavery of Europeans into Egypt by bringing Mamluk (owned) Circassians and Turks from the Black Sea region.

1250–1382   Bahri Mamluks were great patrons of architecture and were responsible for building huge fortresses and mosques.

1382–1517   Circassian Mamluks came into power in 1382 and immediately tried to consolidate their power over the country. The Circassians levied heavy taxes on the population to finance wars against the Mongols in Syria.

1517–1798   Ottoman Turks established their control over the country and sent Pashawat from Istanbul to rule over Egypt.

1798–1801   The French Expedition entered the country under Napoleon Bonaparte to introduce French rule. Dominic-Vivant Denon directed the recording of Egyptian antiquities and monuments resulting in the encyclopedic *Description of Egypt*.

1801–1805   Ottoman Rule restored with the aid and influence of Great Britain.

1805–1848   Muhammad Ali Pasha, the Albanian conqueror, rules Egypt with an iron fist and creates new institutions.

1848–1854   Abbas I, the grandson of Muhammad Ali, became king. His leadership was inconsistent. He closed schools, stopped building roads and railways, and stopped the moves toward industrial development begun under Muhammad Ali.

1854–1863   Said Pasha succeeds to the throne and reversed many of his father's policies and set about to develop the infrastructure much like his great-grandfather had done. He initiated the building of the Suez Canal.

1863–1879   Ismail Pasha was proclaimed Ottoman viceroy on the death of his uncle. He was considered a progressive leader, and completed the building of the Suez Canal in 1869. The rule of Khedive Ismail was progressive. He continued to build the civil infrastructure and the industrial factories.

1879–1892   Tewfik Pasha, Ismail Pasha's son, was pressured to hand over financial management of the nation to Great Britain.

In response, the nationalists forced him to appoint their leader Ahmed Orabi as Minister of War. The English reaction to this move on the part of the nationalists was swift, brutal, and decisive. They defeated Orabi's army at Tel El Kabir and shelled both Alexandria and Ismailiyya.

1892–1952 British Occupation and puppet rulers. All leaders of the nation after Tewfik were under the control of the British government until the 1952 revolution.

1892–1914 Abbas Hilmi Pasha (Abbas II) was a puppet of the British government who tried to lead an independent path. He was the son of Tewfik but quickly sought to make Egypt independent of European influence. He was dethroned by the British in 1914.

1914–1917 Hussein Kamel was made king with British support. This was a difficult period for Egypt because of the unrest among the population owing to the overlordship of the British. Kamel was unable to control the people.

1917–1936 Fouad I was made king with the blessings of the British. Soon after, a power struggle broke out between the king and the people. The Wafd Party succeeded in amassing a large following among the ordinary Egyptians.

1936–1952 Farouk I, the son of Fouad I, ascended the throne. He was greeted with enthusiasm because the people were impressed that he was the first ruler, and the only descendant of the Albanian dynasty of Muhammad Ali Pasha, to speak fluent Arabic.

1952–1970 Gamal Abdel Nasser becomes the first Arab to rule Egypt since the conquest of the country. Known as the "Father of the Nation," he is responsible for building the Aswan High Dam.

1970–1981 Anwar Sadat succeeded Nasser and moved Egypt into a peace agreement with Israel. Considered one of the great statespersons of the era, Sadat sought to break out of the old pattern of hatred between Arabs and Jews.

1981–Present Hosni Muhammad Mubarak, as President of Egypt, has ruled the country longer than any contemporary leader. He has brought relative stability and prosperity to the country as well as expanded educational opportunities.

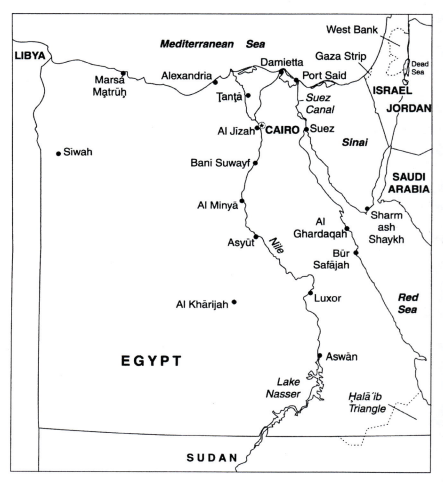

Egypt Overview Map

1

Land, People, and Historical Overview

EGYPT occupies 1,001,450 square miles in the northeast quadrant of the African continent. It is about three times the size of the state of New Mexico in the United States. Egypt is the second most populous nation in Africa, after Nigeria. It is a country defined by a long, powerful river—the storied Nile—flowing south to north. There are ancient river towns lining its banks as well as newer ones built since the harnessing of the river by the Aswan High Dam.

With nearly 1,865 miles of coastline along the Mediterranean and Red seas, Egypt plays a vital role in international trade for the region. Furthermore, it has a long land border that adjoins four countries: 791 miles with Sudan to the south, 715 miles with Libya to the west, and 165 miles with Israel and the Palestinian Authority's Gaza Strip to the east.

Egypt is a country of extremely fertile soil. Many varieties of fruits and vegetables grow in the rich alluvial soil, a legacy of the millennia of inundations that have made the country one vast garden along the Nile. Of course, the vast majority of the land area is in the desert. Thus, Egypt could be defined as a desert penetrated by a river.

The history of Egypt is as complex as it is intriguing; the modern history is almost as riveting as the ancient history. Egypt's modern history is a long narrative of political, social, and cultural experiences in a narrow valley in the middle of a desert. The people who have conquered every inch of fertile soil along the banks of the Nile and made history in a succession of political realities are to be credited with bringing a deeply ancient society into the modern era.

Sailboat (*felucca*) on the Nile

THE LAND

Egypt is essentially two lands, as the ancient name "Ta-wy" emphasizes.[1] On the one hand it is a hot, dry desert, and on the other hand, a verdant, fertile, green strip of land that is bordered by the Damietta River on the east side, the Rosetta River on the west side making the delta, and carrying the mighty river Nile to the Mediterranean Sea. Thus, one might say that the terrain of Egypt is a vast desert plateau bisected by the Nile Valley. To the east of the Nile is the mountainous Eastern (Arabian) Desert, to the west is the Western (Libyan) Desert, which is flatter and whose Qattara Depression is considered the boundary of the great Sahara Desert. To the northeast, Egypt has the Sinai Peninsula where the terrain is split between flat sand desert to the north and high mountains to the south. The highest point in Egypt, Gebel Katrina (Mt. Katherine) at 8,654 high, is located in this region. Like other nations, Egypt has established maritime legal boundaries: 24 nautical miles of a contiguous zone, an exclusive economic zone of 200 nautical miles, and a territorial sea claim of 12 nautical miles. Egypt also has a continental shelf claim of 656 feet in depth or the depth of exploitation.

Hilltop village overlooking the Nile

Height of Major Mountains

Katrina	8,654 ft
Abu-Remail	8,607 ft
Om-Shoumer	8,482 ft
Moussa	7,492 ft
Abu al-Hassan	5,110 ft
Al-Sebaie	4,866 ft

The climate in Egypt is uniformly hot. The summers are dry and hot and the winters are moderate and can be hot in the south. Actually, many Egyptians like to go to Aswan during the winter because of the heat. The vast desert plateau, interrupted by the Nile River, is usually thought of as two deserts: the Eastern Desert and the Western Desert, which is actually a part of the Sahara Desert.

The country is a miracle of land use. Only 3 percent of the land is arable and there are no forests or woodlands nor significant meadows and pastures. Perhaps 2 percent of the land is used for permanent crops and yet the country has been able to support itself with food crops.

Oasis

Natural resources are mainly iron ore, phosphates, manganese, limestone, gypsum, talc, asbestos, lead, zinc, natural gas, and petroleum. One of the hot spots of the international political scene is the boundary dispute between Egypt and Sudan. The administrative border with Sudan does not coincide with the international boundary creating an area called the Hala'ib Triangle, nearly 7,946 square miles of barren land that some experts claim may contain minerals.[2]

Among the issues that have been discussed by the high government officials of Egypt are the environmental crises that are rapidly developing throughout the country. For example, there is some concern that oil pollution is threatening the coral reefs, marine habitats, and tourist beaches. But there are also problems with rapid urbanization, particularly around Cairo, where scarce agricultural lands are being lost to apartment complexes. Furthermore, there is the major issue of the increasing levels of salt in the soil found downstream from the Aswan High Dam. This is the result of the dam (*khazaan*) preventing the natural flow of topsoil from the Upper Nile region, something that had happened for millions of years prior to the construction of the dam. With an increasing population and an intensive use of the arable land, there is some fear that water pollution from agricultural pesticides could become a problem in the future. Pollutants such as raw sewage and industrial effluents could eventually spoil the only freshwater resource of the country: the Nile. All along the Nile, the large industrial centers are using the river for drinking water, sewage, and agriculture. With the possibility that Ethiopia and Sudan, as now planned, will create new dams on the Nile closer to the headwaters, the Egyptian portion of the Nile will be even more threatened by pollution.

In addition to these manmade hazards, there are some natural hazards such as periodic droughts, flash floods caused by infrequent rains, landslides, volcanic activity, and the hot, fierce, dry windstorm called *khamsin* that occurs in the spring. There are also sandstorms (disturbances that cause blinding sand to swirl so that one cannot see more than ten feet ahead), and dust storms that result in fine sand or dust entering every crevice of homes and businesses. But the *khamsin* is a hot and dry wind that can burn the skin; it is like opening the door of an oven and feeling the heat against one's skin. During the period of the hot and dry winds people try to remain in their homes as much as possible. Those homes that are built of mud and adobe tend to have cooler interiors than those made of synthetic materials.

Egypt controls the Sinai Peninsula, the only land bridge between Africa and Asia. It also operates the Suez Canal, the shortest link between the Mediterranean Sea ports and the Indian Ocean ports in Africa and Asia. The geopolitical position of Egypt is important as a nation that deals with the issues of southwest Asia as well as with North Africa. Furthermore, since Egypt is the largest and most important country in the Arab world, it is the center of Arabic culture. Some of the major institutions of the Arabic world are located in Cairo and other Egyptian cities.

Egypt is also a major player in the politics of the African continent because of its integral relationship with the geographic and political issues of the continent and because of its long involvement in the affairs of the continent. From the early days of the political and cultural relationship between Gamal Abdel Nasser of Egypt, Kwame Nkrumah of Ghana, and Haile Selassie of Ethiopia, Egypt has always played an important role in the Organization of African Unity. There are, however, some Egyptians who would like to consider Egypt a part of the Middle East instead of a part of Africa. They are usually influenced by the cultural relationships between the Arab people of the region and place little value in the geographical location of Egypt or its historical relationship to other African cultures long before the domination of Arabic culture. It is like Mexico saying that it has a closer relationship with Spain than it does its North American neighbors, such as the United States and Canada, because of cultural ties. Thus, Egypt can sometimes appear to have a split personality between its African history and location and its Arab culture and religion.

Man holding ancient Ankh symbol

THE PEOPLE

The population of Egypt is estimated to be 90 million by 2005. In 1960, it was 28 million. The growth rate has been increasing each year; currently, there are 29 births for every 1,000 people. At birth, there is an average life expectancy of 61 years: females have a life expectancy of 63 years, and males have a life expectancy of 59 years. It is estimated that the total fertility rate of women is 3.67 children. However, the birth rate is expected to fall. The country's planners are seeking a birth rate of 1.6 percent by 2015. At the present time about 36 percent of the population is below the age of fourteen. Around 97 percent of the Egyptian people live in the Nile Valley and Delta. People are moving to the urban centers of Cairo and Alexandria, as well as others, at an increasing rate because an estimated 47 percent of Egypt's economic and social establishments are in the Cairo and Alexandria political regions, which host 23 percent of the labor force. As of 2001, 44 percent of the population lived in urban areas.

The Egyptian population is comprised of people whose ancestry reaches back to the ancient Egyptians, Arabs, Turks, Bedouins, Berbers, Nubians, Armenians, Albanians, Italians, French, and Greeks. All of these people have had an impact on the making of modern Egypt. The religion of the people is mainly Sunni Muslim. (A Sunni Muslim is one who believes in customary succession.) Literacy is about 48 percent for Egyptians over the age of 15. Male literacy is about twice that of females.

The labor force is comprised of nearly 20 million people, with 36 percent of them working in the government and public sector including the armed forces, 34 percent in agriculture, and about 20 percent in service and manufacturing enterprises. Since there are nearly three million Egyptians working in the Gulf Arab States and Saudi Arabia, there is a shortage of skilled labor for the developing industries of the country.

The Egyptian Nationality

Today, to say that one is an Egyptian means something totally different than it did in ancient times. During the reign of Ramses II, it meant that a person had a certain phenotype and perhaps genotype. It could further be determined that if the person were an Egyptian, then he or she spoke the Egyptian language, which was called "the Divine Speech." All ancient Egyptians believed in a cosmology, a set of values, and a cluster of ideas that made them Egyptian rather than Ethiopian or Greek. This was the model of the Egyptian known throughout history.

However, the modern term "Egyptian" does not refer to a particular genotype, phenotype, or language; rather it is a nationality comprised of many different people who participate in one general Arabized culture. This is true even if a modern-day Egyptian is actually a descendant of Alexandrine Greeks or Aswan Nubians. In reality, to be Egyptian is like being American; it is an idea not necessarily tied to any particular phenotype or genotype but, rather, to one's citizenship. To some degree, Egyptians of Arab descent, that is, with origins in Arabia, have taken the term "Egyptian" to refer to them rather than to the original Egyptian stock, which is primarily now captured in the Nubian and Coptic groups.

Given all the complexity of being Egyptian, one might think that there is no common ground to the nationality. This would be a mistake. Egyptians, of all shades and descents, are rather proud to be called Egyptian. Over the centuries the people have been molded, especially during the modern era, by the Islamic religion into one common people. While it is still true that one can find numerous heritages among the diverse populations of Egyptians, it is a fact that the Arab culture as defined by the religion of Islam is the dominant definer of manners, protocol, etiquette, attitudes, and behaviors.

Thus, the modern culture of Egypt is predominantly influenced by Islam, but there is evidence of the rich traditions of the Nubian, Greek, Turk, and Albanian people as well. Add to this mixture the political and cultural strands of the British, Mamluk (Egyptian military class that occupied the Sultanate from 1250 to 1517), and French rulers over the years, and the complexity of Egypt's modern national composition is even greater.

The Nubian Heritage

Nubians are an ancient people, perhaps the oldest people of the Nile Valley in Egypt to retain a definite sense of their own culture. Unlike the people who refer to themselves as Egyptians, the Nubians have sought to remain as unmixed as possible to the extent that they speak their own languages and have often refused to have them written down.

The legacy of the Nubians is extensive. In fact, the Nubians are modern Egypt's most authentic reminders of the ancient Egyptian ways of agriculture, including planting, harvesting, and food preparation. In addition, the Nubians have maintained the closest affiliation with the ancient Egyptian way of house construction. When one sees the Nubian houses of modern Egypt, one is looking back into time at the way the early Egyptians constructed their homes out of the mud and straw they found along the banks of the Nile. It has been noted that the modern Nubians "had no contractors, engineers, or architects to help them. If they managed, it was mainly because they had retained a technique for roofing in mud brick, using vaults and domes, which had been passed down to them from their forefathers, the Ancient Egyptians" (Hassan Fathy, El-Hakim in 1999, p. 4). Of course the Nubians may not have had trained engineers or contractors but they had the knowledge of their ancient past.

Modern Egyptians look to the Nubians for inspiration and spirituality. They frequently speak of the Nubians in the same way the ancient Greeks spoke of them, as the "straightest of men." They believe that the Nubians represent the oldest traditions of the Nile Valley as demonstrated in their rituals, their architecture, and their homes. There are three main groups of Nubians in Egypt: the Kanuz, Mahas, and Matoki.[3] Even today the Nubians of Elephantine Island in the Nile River near Aswan tell of their memories of the ancient days. A day in the life of the Nubian on Elephantine begins before the sun rises. The early morning prayers are a must for the devout Muslim Nubians. Most Nubians now consider themselves Islamic, although there are a few who hold to the Christian beliefs that existed prior to the Muslims' conquest. Still others refer to themselves as traditionalists, believing in the ancient gods of Nubia.

With the construction of the Aswan High Dam—begun in June 1964 and completed in 1968—and the imminent flooding of the Nubian homeland, the last of the Nubian people were forced to leave the area that extended south along the banks of the Nile from Aswan in the north to the Sudanese border nearly 290 miles south. It is estimated that 150,000 Nubians were relocated north of Aswan between the cities of Esna and Kom Ombo. Across the border in Sudan, Nubians were relocated to the banks of the Atbara River, more than 600 miles from where they lived.

The creation of the Aswan High Dam changed the entire geography of the Nubian homeland. Arable land, long cultivated for date palms used for export, was now beneath the huge Lake Nasser with a surface area of 2,317 square miles. Nubians have been affected by every one of the dams built along the Nile. Between 1899 and 1902, the British built a dam a few miles upstream from Aswan. At a height of 100 feet, this dam created a lake that flooded the Nile Valley for 140 miles and raised the water level of what had been the river from 285 feet to 348 feet, permanently wiping out the area of the Nubian Kanuz people. Of course, this change in the geography had enormous effects on the Nubian people. They had to move to areas north or south of their ancient homeland. The government of the day had little sympathy for them. In fact, the British built the dam, and the government, largely under the influence of the British, agreed after protests to assist and compensate the Nubians for their lands.

There were three proposals. The first was to allot government land north of Aswan. The dislocated Nubians would have to purchase this land. Second, the government would survey and appraise lands that could be reclaimed from the desert for the Nubians. The people could receive this drained and irrigated land for little or nothing. Third, the Nubians could receive a cash indemnity to a value of no more than 50 percent of the original value of the lands flooded. Some of the people who lost their homes and fertile lands to the early dam and its enhancement in the 1930s did not receive their compensation until 1964, thirty-one years after the claim had been made and many years after some of the older family members had died (El-Hakim 1993, 9).

During the 1960s the government provided pumps and irrigation assistance for the Nubians, who had largely lost their agricultural livelihood because of the flooding of their date palm groves. The people had been impoverished by the first dam and were further impoverished when the able-bodied young men left the rural areas for Aswan in search of work after the Aswan High Dam was built. Although the people were relocated, many of the men decided to leave their wives at home in the resettlement camps in order to make money working in the cities.

The Nubians have been characterized as "a refined and dignified people, the possessors of an ancient culture with social traditions, customs and languages distinct from the rest of Egypt" (El-Hakim 1993, 10). They have distinct customs and traditions because they are not Arabs. Their history in

Egypt predates that of the largely Arab population of present-day Egypt and goes back to the days of pharaonic Egypt. In one sense the building of the Aswan High Dam ended the narrative life of the Nubian people. They had been dislocated, relocated, and their history disrupted and interrupted by a number of Egyptian governments.

Today, the condition of the Nubians who live north of Aswan is improving economically as they enter the tourist industry in numerous capacities. They are star sailors and have nearly monopolized the motorized boat and sailboat (*feluccas*) business on the Nile River at Aswan. Some villages are more prosperous than others owing to their proximity to the large numbers of tourists who visit the country each year. Others are eking out a living raising tomatoes, corn, millet, and clay beans. One gets the impression that Nubia will live on, but the rich heritage of the culture in temples, tombs, and the old villages are forever buried beneath one of the largest manmade lakes in the world.

The Greek Presence

When Alexander the Macedonian (the Great) conquered Egypt in 332 B.C.E., he left his general Ptolemy in charge of the newly won territory. Subsequent generations of Ptolemy's descendants went a long way toward making the area around Alexandria Greek in character. Alexandria had been founded on the site of the ancient town of Rakoda, sometimes written Rhacotis, and increasingly took on a Greek character. At one time Alexandria, although in Africa, was called the greatest of the Greek cities. It had been made that way by the gathering of men and women from the Greek world to study and engage in commerce. A port city, Alexandria became the ears and eyes of the Greeks to the work and activities of the Africans, but it was also the city through which many ideas from the African interior reached the wider world of Europe and Asia.

The relationship between ancient Egypt and ancient Greece is very close. Egypt, of course, was old before there was a Greece. However, soon after Homer wrote the *Iliad*, history records that many Greeks, including the first Greek philosophers—Thales, Isocrates, and Pythagoras—studied in Egypt. Nevertheless, the Greeks were destined to conquer Egypt and, in their conquest, to make Alexandria a famous Mediterranean city.

One encounters the presence of Greece in modern Egypt in the city of Alexandria as well as in the artistic and cultural life of the country. From the Coptic language—ancient Egyptian written with Greek characters—to many influences on drama, painting, and music, Greece finds its way into the modern consciousness of Egypt.

GENERAL HISTORY

No nation has as long a continuous history as Egypt. A writer could very easily start a discussion of its history from the uniting of the "Two Lands" by King Menes around 3100 B.C.E. and end in 2500 B.C.E. at the building of the great pyramids and you would have covered more time than it has been from Columbus' first voyage to the New World to the present time. The objective of this work is the culture and customs of modern Egypt. But what is the meaning of modern Egypt given its long history?

Some writers have declared that the most significant date in Egyptian history since the fall of the pharaohs is 641 C.E. This was the date when the Arabs consolidated their conquest of the country. After the death of the Prophet Muhammad, the followers of Islam left Arabia and went into many neighboring countries with the words of the prophet. They were able to conquer Egypt with little opposition, grafting onto the fundamental African identity of Egypt an Arab character and the Arabic language. Egypt was to be brought into the Islamic sphere of the world.

Prior to the coming of the Arabs, the native inhabitants of the country had been Africans, mainly of Bedouin and Nubian stock, and Greek Christian Copts, using their own language as a legacy of the ancient Egyptian language. The Greeks had settled in Egypt in numbers after the Macedonian conquest in 332 B.C.E. They had initially adopted the Egyptian religion but became the leaders of the new Christian ideology when it first appeared in Alexandria. The Greeks later resisted Islam as a faith and Arabic as a culture. However, it would not be long before the country would be completely dominated by the Arabic culture brought to the land from Arabia by General El As and those who followed him.

There are several significant periods in modern Egyptian history. Our discussion of Egyptian culture and customs must begin with the Fatimid Period in 969 C.E. After the Fatimid Period, there are several proper divisions of the history of the country in the modern age. Each one will be discussed as a contribution to the present-day Egypt. It is the Islamic culture that has made modern Egyptian history, and one cannot understand the country without a proper appreciation of the emergence of that culture in the lives of the people (see also Chapter 3, "Religion and Worldview").

The Birth of Muhammad

In about the year 570 C.E., a child who would be named Muhammad was born to a family belonging to a clan of Quraysh, the ruling group of Mecca, a city in the Hijaz region of northwestern Arabia. Muhammad would be the founder of Islam, and his followers would have a great influence on Egypt. Mecca was the original site of an ancient shrine called the Kabbah. Because of the many merchants from Ethiopia, Kemet, Greece, and Byzantine, it had become one of the principal cities of southwest Asia.

Muhammad's father, Abdel Allah ibn Abdel al-Muttalib, died before the child was born. His mother, Aminah, died when he was six years old. The orphaned child was consigned to the care of his grandfather who headed the Hashim clan. Soon after the death of his grandfather, Muhammad was sent to his Uncle Abu Talib, who sent him, as was customary, to live with a Bedouin family for two years. This custom was followed by the noble families of Mecca, Medina, Tayif, and other towns of the Hijaz so that the young boy could undergo hardships and learn suffering. He mastered the language of the Arabs, who considered their language their proudest contribution. He shared and endured the lessons of the environment with the Arabs who lived in tents in the deserts. He soon appreciated the quality of their lives.

When he was in his twenties, Muhammad entered the service of a widow named Khadijah as a merchant, actively trading with caravans. Soon he married her and they had two sons, both of whom died. They then had four daughters.

During this period Muhammad traveled widely. By the time he was in his forties he had decided to meditate and reflect on the ways of men. He would go to a cave on Mount Hira, outside of Mecca, to meditate. One day as he sat in the cave he heard a voice that told him the voice belonged to the archangel Gabriel and asked him to recite the following words: "In the name of thy Lord who created man from a clot of blood." Three times Muhammad said "no," and each time he said "no" the voice would repeat the instructions. Finally, he recited the words that became the first five verses of the ninety-sixth chapter, or *sura*, of the Qur'an (the sacred text of Islam)—proclaiming that God is the creator and source of humans' and all knowledge.

These experiences taught Muhammad that he had to preach. He started with his family and then proclaimed the words to the merchants of the Quraysh clan. Some accepted his words and followed him; others rejected his words and opposed his message. The opposition served to make him sharpen his arguments, and he became a great debater against paganism. The belief of the unity of God was supreme in his teaching. Because the Qur'an rejected polytheism and emphasized moral obligations, it represented a serious challenge to the people of Mecca.

After Muhammad had preached for about ten years, the opposition was ready to do bodily harm to him and his followers. He sent some of his followers to the country of Ethiopia where they were received and protected by the Christian king of that land. Soon the enemies of Muhammad came after him. While he sent some of his followers ahead to Medina, he stayed back until the plot to kill him and his closest friend, Abu Bakr, became quite clear. He then left his cousin, Ali, in his bed and journeyed with Abu Bakr toward Medina to catch up with the other emigrants. They stopped in a cave. A spider spun its web across the entry to the cave, and when the pursuers saw that the web was unbroken, they ceased searching for Muhammad and Abu Bakr. They then set out for Medina and were welcomed by a throng of followers. This period was called the Hegira, or "Flight to Medina." It is this date in the fall of 622 C.E. that is usually given as the date for the beginning of Islam. The Hegira was not a flight but a carefully planned migration that marks the beginning of Islam and a decisive break with the past. Those who made the trip from Mecca to Medina were called the *Muhajirun* (the emigrants), while those who helped in Medina were called the *Ansar* (helpers).

The Fatimid Period, 969–1171

The name "Fatimid" is derived from the fact that the leaders of this period trace their origins to Fatimah az-Zahra, the daughter of the Prophet Muhammad, and her husband, Ali ibn Abu Talib. The Fatimid Dynasty embraced the Shi'a (Partisans of Ali) doctrines that rejected the first three caliphs (a successor of Muhammad) of Islam—Abu Bakr, Omar, and Uthman—believing that they had usurped the legitimate succession from Ali.

Initially, the Shi'a were loyal Muslims who just questioned the fact that Ali had been bypassed for leadership. However, when Ali and his sons—Hassan and Hussein—were assassinated, the division hardened and the Shi'a Dynasty separated itself from the Sunni caliphate and established their own caliphate. The conquest of Egypt in 969 C.E. gave the Shi'a an important center for extending their domination over the rest of northern Africa. They offered the possibility of a *mahdi* (an infallible ruler). The *mahdi* was not to be a return of Ali, but one who would bring to Islam a restoration of hope and optimism at the end of the tenth century. Visions of the *mahdi* and expressions of his coming to the world were similar to the Christian idea of the return of Jesus Christ. There was an anticipation that a new beginning would arrive when the infallible ruler appeared to the faithful.

The Shiites established their political seat in the new imperial capital al-Qahira (Cairo) which means "the Triumphant." They built lavish palaces and beautiful temples inside the walls of the city. In addition, they established the Al-Azhar Mosque and its university that is the oldest existing institution of higher learning. So the Fatimids must be considered the artistic and intellectual innovators in the emergent Egypt of modern times.

How the Fatimids, descendants of Ali and Fatimah (therefore Fatimid), could create a dynasty after the incredible history of intrigue and dissimulation that had already occurred in the Islamic world is itself a story worthy of retelling because it is at the heart of what makes Egypt so appealing today. They came at a time in the history of the country when the people awaited leadership that would bring stability and progress, two elements essential for modernity.

Obaidallah, a man of Persian extraction, and ostensibly the great grandson of Ismail Pasha, himself a descendant of Ali and Fatimah, is the key personality in the rise of Shi'a, but he is not the man responsible for the advancement of Shi'a faith. This credit goes to another Persian named al-Shi'a (the Shiite–Muslim believes in Ali's succession to Muhammed) for his enthusiasm and faith in the cause. He was one of the greatest propagandists of all times. Al-Shi'a lived during the time when there were no newspapers, no television, and no Internet, but there was the annual *hajj* (pilgrimage) to Mecca. Hundreds of thousands of pilgrims came from all over the world to Mecca every year as their sacred *hajj*. Where else could one find so many people devoted to the cause of Islam? Where else could one find people who would know the story of the daughter of the prophet, Fatimah and her husband, Ali?

Al-Shi'a found the pilgrims who had suffered greatly to make the costly journey to Mecca ready to hear the words that he spoke. He was quite successful with some groups of Berbers from Algeria who invited him to return with them to Algeria to teach the Qur'an. When they reached their rugged mountain region they elected him leader of the group. Al-Shi'a was the spiritual leader as well as the military and political head of a vigorous band of Berbers. Once he had established his presence strongly in Algeria, he sent for Obaidallah. Reaching Tripoli, Obaidallah was captured and imprisoned by the orthodox dynasty ruling Tunisia. But three years later he was rescued by the military cunning of al-Shi'a. On August 26, 909, al-Shi'a presented Obaidallah to a vast crowd of warriors as the anticipated *mahdi*. The price he was to pay for introducing his friend as the infallible ruler was his own death two years later. Al-Shi'a could not remain the major and preeminent teacher of Islam among the Berbers if Obaidallah was indeed the *mahdi*. Soon a fierce rivalry began between the two Persians, which resulted in Obaidallah emerging as the most authoritative voice of Islam. He then set about ridding himself of rivals, and al-Shi'a was killed.

A new city was laid out on a promontory of eastern Tunisia and named Mahdia. Some scholars believe that it was to be the model for the new capital of Egypt once the Shiites captured the country. Talk of the conquest of Egypt was intense. Preparations for the taking of the country went on for months. It is believed that a Jewish convert to Islam, Yakub ibn Killis, had a lot to do with the conquest of Egypt. He was able to give precise facts about the conditions inside Egypt to the leaders in Tunisia. Although the Fatimids had attacked Egypt on several occasions and in 914 their fleet had captured Alexandria, they were not yet ready to take the entire country. Ibn Killis told the leaders in Tunisia that many people inside Egypt were looking for a descendant of Ali to bring deliverance to them. By this time Islam had roots in Egypt that went back to the seventh century C.E. Many followers of the religion had come to believe that Fatimah and Abu were the true carriers of the Prophet Muhammad's legacy, and therefore they believed in the Shiite doctrine. What was needed was a *mahdi*, and the Fatimids would give them what they asked.

Al-Mo'izz, the Fatimid leader, put an army of 100,000 men at the disposal of a converted Greek named Gohar. Leaving Tunisia in February 969, he landed in Alexandria and occupied the city. By July, Gohar's Fatimid army had reached Giza. They were aided by the fact that a plague had devastated much of the army of Egypt, who had lost nearly half a million people. When the battle started, the city of Cairo threw itself on the mercy of the military leader. He gave the city complete amnesty and forbade his soldiers to loot. Soon he invited al-Mo'izz to enter his new city. When he came to Cairo, al-Mu'izz preached a sermon at the Al-Azhar Mosque as an indication of his new position as spiritual leader. He supervised construction, paid his soldiers well, and created a shipbuilding industry. Al-Mo'izz changed the name of al-Mansuriya to al-Qahira or Cairo. It is from this time and because of this fact that we are able to say that modern Egypt begins in 969 with the Fatimids.

The fact that the people did not have to pay taxes to Iraq but to their own caliphs made a lot of sense to the Egyptians. Their money remained in the country. When al-Mo'izz died after about two years, his son al-Aziz came to power. Al-Aziz ruled from 975 to 990. With all that they were doing, the Fatimids were not able to convince the country to become Shi'a. The old Muslims kept to the Sunni tradition believing in the lineage of Abu Bakr, the Prophet's uncle. But the long-term effect of the inability of the Fatimids to convert the country to Shi'a meant that Egypt was estranged from the eastern part of the Islamic world where most people found the caliphate of Baghdad the legitimate authority of the Muslim people. Yet in fifteen years the Fatimids had made Cairo the most important city in the Islamic world; indeed, in the tenth century this meant the most important city in the world.

Furthermore, the nation of Egypt prospered under the leadership of the Fatimids. The opening of the country to the West created opportunities that had not existed before for commercial and cultural interaction. This was not the first time that Europeans and Muslims had met, but it was probably the first time that they had met with a respect for each other. However, the fact that the Fatimids could not trust their fellow Muslims meant that they turned more toward Jews, Copts, Greeks, and Armenians for service in their administration. They were, like so many rulers of Egypt before and after, an insurgent group who brought foreigners who had no organic relationship with the people into the body politic of the country. Thus, they often kept their own counsel, defying the rigid prohibitions of other Muslims, enjoying feasting and wine drinking offered by the Christian monks. They ruled the country from a distance, remaining behind their walls until the rule of Caliph al-Hakim, the demented.

Al-Aziz's son by a Greek concubine, the sister of the two Greek Orthodox bishops, was born al-Hakim on August 14, 985. Al-Aziz died when the young boy was eleven. Given a tutor, Burjuwan, a Slav, the young al-Hakim was soon given the eloquent name, al-Hakim bi-Amrih Allah ("he who rules at the command of God"). With al-Hakim's kingship, the Fatimids soon declined. He began his rule by building a lovely mosque and occasionally leaving the palace to mingle with the people. Soon, however, he became a tyrant, ruling with something of an insane caprice. He killed those whom he disliked and made decrees that indicated his demented state. By the time he was fifteen he had murdered Burjuwan. He made it a crime punishable by death for anyone to work during the day. His nocturnal interests were reflected in the establishment of a council for the night. However, he soon tired of the council and made his control over the city and the state the only dictate that mattered. His entourage dreaded his voice, his presence, and his actions. In addition to murdering Burjuwan, he killed several ministers of state. Believing that women should stay indoors twenty-four hours a day and thinking that without shoes they would not be able to walk on the manure-strewn streets of Cairo, al-Hakim prohibited the manufacture of women shoes. In addition, he banned the consumption of *molokhiya* (a spinachlike vegetable), which was a staple of the Egyptian diet.

Al-Hakim is one of the most complex personalities in modern Egyptian history. He persecuted all types of people and humiliated Arab merchants in the markets but left his most vicious attacks for the Christian community, even though his mother and uncles were Christians. In fact, "Copts were placed under many indignities, such as having to wear a heavy cross if they went to a public bath. In 1010, as part of his mania against Christians, he first had the church of the Holy Sepulcher in Jerusalem destroyed and then gave the custody of the Holy Places to the Greek Church of his mother instead of the Latin or Roman Church of western Europe" (Stewart 1996, 68). Actually, in a remote way this action was a pretext for the First Crusade later in the century. Christians in the West would give up their earthly possessions to join long and arduous adventures to the East to rescue the holy places from the Eastern Church or the Muslims.

While al-Hakim's rule did not bring about any wholesale conversion to

Shi'a, he did create, in the interstices between insanity and prudence, an atmosphere for intellectual discussion within the regime. The House of Science that he established for learned men to discuss all manner of subjects became one of the freest places of knowledge in the world at the time. His library, an intellectual arsenal, was the greatest collection of manuscripts in Arabic at the time; and an observatory, meticulously built with equipment designed for scientific research, was the precursor to more modern technologies in observatories. Thus, this strange, brutal, and mad ruler, whose Shiite theories did not fly in Egypt, brought the intellectual discussions to a new level.

Two Persians—Hamzah and al-Durzi—migrated to Cairo because of the intellectual debates about the religion and began preaching the divinity of al-Hakim. When a group of their followers entered a mosque and demanded that the orthodox Muslim judge read a text that began with the *Bismillah*— "In the name of al Hakim billah, the merciful, the compassionate" instead of the normal "In the name of Allah, the merciful, the compassionate"—the faithful could not take it any longer. They took stones and killed the three Shiites on the spot. Al-Hakim, in a murderous rage, sent Nubian, Turkish, and Berber troops into the city to destroy the shops of Arab merchants whom he accused of promoting the disrespect for his rule.

Al-Hakim's reign ended mysteriously. He rode his favorite mule named "the Moon" up into the Mokattam hills one evening and vanished. The mule was found but al-Hakim was never found. Many people believed that he had been murdered by bandits from the City of the Dead, the large cemetery outside the palace walls.

In 1047, when the Persian scholar Nasir Khosram visited Cairo, the caliph in power was al-Mostansir, the grandson of al-Hakim. His mother was a black Egyptian, and although his father was of Persian–Greek ancestry, al-Mostansir was a partisan to the Egyptian social and political order. According to Nasir, al-Mostansir's government would be plagued by disturbances between the African-born black and European-born white guards in the palace. Al-Mostansir's preference for the black guards created an unstable situation in his court, which did not abate for several years. Yet al-Mostansir presided over the greatest period in Fatimid history in Egypt. The markets were full of vegetables and the streets were bustling with activity. Indeed, the account of Nasir brings alive the city and state during the eleventh century. He claims that shopkeepers did not have to lock their shops and no one would dare to steal. Al-Mostansir had an impressive army, comprised of troops from Nubia, Ethiopia, Turkey, Persia, Arabia, and the Slav lands. Fatimid Egypt at this time was the most excellent symbol of Islam. Soon after al-Mostansir, the Fatimid rule would see a steep decline.

Even so, the Fatimids continued to rule Egypt for 150 years until the

Seljuk Sultan Nureddin sent an expedition to overthrow the Fatimids. His nephew Salah ad-Din al-Ayyubi captured Alexandria and set the stage for the Ayyubid Dynasty.

The Ayyubid Rule, 1171–1250

Salah ad-Din al-Ayyubi (Saladin) became the Egyptian leader after the death of the last Fatimid caliph in 1171. When the Crusaders entered the African continent and laid waste to parts of Cairo, Saladin built fortifications and erected the Citadel. He was able to defeat the Christian armies and their Nubian allies. His reign is remembered as one of the most important in the history of Egypt because of his humility and courage, as well as his military and administrative discipline.

Saladin reigned for twenty-four years. He spent eight years of his reign in Cairo during which time he established schools, built hospitals, and improved the infrastructure of the city. He introduced slavery of Europeans into Egypt by bringing Mamluk (owned) Circassians and Turks from the Black Sea region. Under his rule the Mamluks were allowed to own land, raise families, and rise to prominence within the society.

In 1193, Saladin died and was succeeded by his brother, al-Adil, after a long succession dispute. When al-Adil died in Syria in 1218, he was succeeded by his son and Saladin's nephew, al-Kamil, who fought back the Fifth Crusade. His successor was Sultan Ayyub who brought in more Mamluks and married a slave girl named Shagarat ad-Durr. When Ayyub died, his wife became the first woman to rule Egypt since Cleopatra. When Shagarat's new husband, Aybak, decided to take a second wife, she had him killed. Soon thereafter she was assassinated, and the Mamluk military commander al-Malik Baybars assumed control over Egypt and ushered in the rule of the Mamluks.

The Mamluk Period, 1250–1517

Al-Malik Baybars I, a Mamluk from the Black Sea region, took over power in Egypt in the midst of turmoil. However, he was not able to establish complete dominance over the country because of the dissension. In the aftermath of the murder of Shagarat ad-Durr, the heirs of Baybars were killed by Qalawun, another Mamluk military leader, who consolidated his rule on Egypt (see the next section).

Qalawun became a great patron of architecture and built many mosques and other buildings in Cairo. He established political and diplomatic relations with many other African nations as well as with European and Asian countries. Qalawun was succeeded by his son Muhammad an-Nasir, who ruled for nearly fifty years (1294–1340). An-Nasir continued his father's interest in building fortresses and mosques.

Under Muhammad an-Nasir the Mamluk armies defeated the Mongols in Syria. The descendants of an-Nasir were neither as astute nor as courageous as he was, and the Turkish Mamluk dynasty gradually lost power. It was succeeded by the Circassian Mamluk under the leadership of Sultan Barquq. The Burgi Mamluk, as they were called after the garrison set beneath the Citadel in Cairo, campaigned against the Mongols to drive them out of all Muslim lands.

The Mamluk Period was not to be without its challenges at home. Heavy taxation to pay for military campaigns created unrest among the population and debilitated the economy. The plague swept through the country during the reign of Barquq's son, Faraj. This was a difficult period for the nation. Nevertheless the Mamluks attempted to continue the campaigns against Mongol intervention in Syria. Sultan Barsbey brought about a revival in Egypt's fortunes. He saw the potential threat from the Ottoman Turks and established good relations with them.

The forty-sixth Mamluk sultan was Qunsah al-Ghuri who saw several disasters. The first was the collapse of the economy that happened because the Europeans started rounding the Cape of Good Hope rather than seeing Cairo as the major trading city in the African and Asian worlds. Sultan Qunsah al-Ghuri was fatally wounded in battle with the Ottoman Turks in 1516. A year later the Ottomans defeated the Mamluks and prepared the way for their rule of Egypt.

The Ottoman Rule, 1517–1798

The Ottoman Rule of Egypt was indirect. They controlled the country from Istanbul and sent Pashawat, trained in Istanbul, to rule Egypt. Since the country had a large number of people of Turkish heritage, including the remnants of the Seljuk Turks, and an overwhelmingly Islamic culture, it was easy to govern. Thousands of slaves were brought into the country from the Caucasus as mercenaries who served the Ottoman governors and military leaders. These Caucasus mercenaries were used to keep the masses of Egyptians under control. It was an effective way of managing the population but a very ineffective system for colonial administration. Although the Ottoman Turks were brilliant military strategists, they proved to be poor colonial administrators. By leaving the daily operations to Pashawat and his minions—many of whom had little understanding of the Egyptian people—the Ottomans encouraged rebellion, unrest, and disrespect for the Ottoman Empire.

There was neglect of the infrastructure and little attention to the social needs of the masses. Ultimately, the deterioration in the social and political situation paved the way for the French invasion of 1798.

The European Conquest, 1798–1801

By striking before the British (their rivals), the French could establish their trade routes to India through Egypt; thus, Napoleon Bonaparte's army crushed the Mamluk armies of the Ottomans at Imbabu in 1798. His intention was to colonize Egypt and create a French-speaking society in the country. Following the pattern of other national and imperial powers, the aim of Napoleon's army was to stake out a claim for France in the ancient land. He immediately established a French administration, taking over from the Ottomans, and implemented many public works to win the allegiance of the Egyptian people, a few of whom believed that the French had liberated them from the inept rule of the Ottomans. The fact that France took a direct hand in running the country—cleaning the streets, creating jobs, clearing blocked irrigation canals, and building bridges—made the French popular among some circles. Napoleon showed respect for Islam and the Qur'an but still most Egyptians were suspicious. Much like the ancient pilgrimage of Alexander to the Siwa Oasis to seek the oracle of Amen-Ra, Napoleon gave verbal service to the glories of Islam hoping to win the support of the people. However, his visionary dreams were grandiose. He stated, "I saw myself founding a religion, marching into Asia, riding an elephant, a turban on my head and in my hand the new Qur'an that I would have composed to suit my needs" (Stewart 1996, 156).

The French efforts at bringing their administration to the country were doomed from the outset. There were many obstacles, including the threat and actuality of international hostilities over the invasion. The British Royal Navy, under Rear Admiral Horatio Nelson, destroyed the French fleet moored at Abu Qir Bay in Alexandria, within a month after it had docked. Furthermore, the sultan of the Ottoman Empire, from his palace in Istanbul, threatened to engage the French in war. Under pressure from home to explain the French invasion and the political dangers to the Grand Army, Napoleon secretly returned to France, leaving his armies in Africa. Soon thereafter, Napoleon's commander, General Jean-Baptiste Kléber, was assassinated by a Syrian, Suliman al-Halabi, who implicated three religious leaders. All four were executed; the three sheikhs were beheaded, and al-Halabi was impaled, after having his right arm burned off with hot tar.

General Jacques-François de Menou, who converted to Islam, took over the leadership of the French forces and declared that Egypt was now a French protectorate. The French worked feverishly to create a class of Egyptians who would be an elite, Western-trained indigenous group. Napoleon had been a student of Comte de Volney, who in 1791 wrote a famous book—translated as *Ruins, or a Survey of the Revolution of Empire*—about the history and people of Egypt. Volney wrote: "How are we astonished . . . when we reflect that to the race of Negroes, at present our slaves, and the objects of our extreme contempt, we owe our arts, sciences, and even the very use of speech, and when we recollect that, in the midst of those nations who call themselves the friends of liberty and humanity, the most barbarous of slaveries is justified" (cited in Cheikh Anta Diop 1991, 66). Stewart correctly assessed Napoleon's attitude when he wrote: "As a disciple of Volney, Napoleon believed that the native-born men of religion, the *ulama*, could provide a basis for social re-vitalization" (1996, 160). This was done to minimize the control of the Mamluks, a white European people from the Caucasus and Georgia, used as mercenaries by the Ottoman Turks.

The diary of the African writer of Somali origin, Abdul Rahman al-Jabarti, a graduate of Al-Azhar University, is the most telling portrait of the invasion and conquest of Cairo by the French. Al-Jabarti claims that the English had warned the people of Alexandria that the French were bringing a large fleet to invade, but the Egyptians did not believe the English and told them to leave their shores (Stewart 1996, 156). The English left and ten days later Napoleon's army was "as thick as locusts in the city" (ibid.). The French soon took over Alexandria, hoisted their flag, and made everyone wear the tricolors of red, blue, and white as an indication of the French conquest. They would soon move on to Cairo. Al-Jabarti, who was in Cairo during the entire episode, described the shock wave that ran throughout the city when it was discovered that the French had defeated the Mamluks and Bed-ouins in Alexandria and was now moving toward Cairo. The leading emirs—Ibrahim Bey and Murad Bey—reported this news to Istanbul in an effort to have the Ottomans, the real rulers of Egypt, get involved in the defense of the country. While Murad Bey was trying to assemble a large army to hold back the French, a clandestine pamphlet appeared in Cairo, allegedly distributed by Coptic Christians. The pamphlet began with the *Bismillah*:

In the name of God, the Merciful, the Compassionate! On behalf of the French nation, founded on liberty and equality, Bonaparte, the great general and commander-in-chief of the French army, proclaims to the entire population of Egypt that for far too long the emirs who rule the country have insulted the French nation and outraged its merchants. The hour of their chastisement has struck. For long centuries this riffraff of slaves purchased in the Caucasus or Georgia have tyrannized the most beautiful country in the world. But God, Master of the Universe and the All-Powerful, has decreed that their reign should cease. People of Egypt! You have been told that I have come here to destroy your religion. It is a lie. Don't believe it. Say to such liars that I am only come among you to seize your rights from the hands of tyrants and restore them to you and that, more than do the Mamluks, I adore God and respect his Prophet and the Qur'an.

Once the French had routed the Mamluks at Imbaba, they moved into the city and took over the palace of Muhammad Bey al-Alfi. The palace had been built the year before at great expense, but Napoleon wasted no time in moving into it. All seemed to go well, the French were in charge, they cleaned the streets, opened the cafés, built irrigation canals, and spent money in the bazaar. However, the expeditionary force waiting in the ships off the coast of Egypt was a sitting duck, cut off from its supply sources and its home base. It would not be long before the French would find this situation dangerous because the British government was looking to make a play on Egypt; in the eyes of the British, the fact that France had won the race to Alexandria did not mean that it would hold the prize for long.

Once the British heard the news that the French had occupied Cairo, they moved to annihilate the French fleet in the Mediterranean. Rear Admiral Nelson, with technologically superior ships and a much better trained group of sailors, began the assault on the French vessels on the evening of August 1, 1798, and by noon the next day, the British had demolished the French navy at Alexandria. The British then moved into Alexandria and alongside the Ottomans, who had declared war on Napoleon, recaptured the cities of Damietta and Cairo. The French were forced to surrender without ever having controlled the entire country.

The ramifications of the French invasion were many for Egypt. But the principal issue was the decline of the Islamic world. The fact that the Ottoman Empire, an Islamic one, could not prevent the Christian nations from conquering a nation under the influence of Islam was a stunning discovery for the Islamic world. In many ways the French army invasion and its initial success over the Mamluk forces shattered the Islamic world's confidence in its ability to fight off the Christian nations.

The Dynasty of Muhammad Ali Pasha, 1801–1892

The Egyptian society underwent an enormous upheaval because of the French invasion and its subsequent defeat by the British. Many political struggles ensued and in the internal battles an Albanian lieutenant in the Ottoman army, Muhammad Ali, became the leader of the most powerful faction. He succeeded in driving the British out of Egypt and he was soon elevated to the position of Khedive (or Viceroy) of Egypt. Of course, the British would return nearly one hundred years later. In the meantime, Muhammad Ali realized that he had a problem with the large numbers of armed Mamluks in the country. Although they were Circassian or Turk, and he, Albanian, Ali believed that the Egyptians could not be free unless they broke the back of the Mamluk mercenaries.

In a spectacular manner, Khedive Ali ended the power and influence of the Mamluks. In the sixth year of his rule, he invited 470 of the top Mamluk soldiers to a banquet at the Citadel. While they were enjoying themselves, he had them all killed. The massacre of the Mamluk officers ended their threat and consolidated the power of the khedive. Once again the Egyptian society was rocked by a major event that brought about transformations of power and prestige. Muhammad Ali, the Albanian, had become the new key figure in the history of Egypt. All the while the Egyptian people were serving as a backdrop to the dramatic political stage occupied by the Turks, Circassians, and Albanians.

From the decisive massacre of the Mamluks to the end of his rule (1848), Muhammad Ali was considered the absolute ruler of Egypt. Nominally he was under the authority of the Ottomans, but Istanbul had almost no effective rights in Egypt during the reign of Muhammad Ali. He was dedicated to the modernization of Egypt and went about building roads, factories, canals, railways, and public buildings. Using his international expertise and the contacts that had been made with Europeans, Ali brought in European architects and technicians to assist in the construction of the country. His aim was to make Egypt a regional power.

Once Ali had gotten the nation involved in reinventing itself, he moved to make his armies powerful. Eventually, Syria, Sudan, Greece, and the Arabian Peninsula fell under his control until 1839. While he paid lip service to the Ottoman caliph in Istanbul, he essentially controlled a large part of the Ottoman Empire himself. The British, acting in the role of international police, tried to prevent Ali from extending his power to other areas of the region. Britain actually forced him to relinquish some of his power to the Ottoman sultan.

When Muhammad Ali died in 1848, his grandson, Abbas, succeeded him. Abbas I's rule was inconsistent. He opened Egypt to free trade, lifting tariffs and making it possible for European nations to enter the Egyptian market. However, he closed schools, stopped building roads and railways, and stopped the moves toward industrial development. Whereas Muhammad Ali had set in motion the process of self-sufficiency, Abbas I effectively called a halt to that movement.

The successor of Abbas I was his son Said Pasha. Fortunately, Said Pasha reversed many of his father's policies and set about to develop the infrastructure much like his great-grandfather had done. He initiated the building of the Suez Canal, which was completed in 1869 by his successor, and nephew, Khedive Ismail. The rule of Khedive Ismail was progressive. He continued to build the civil infrastructure and the industrial factories. In fact, he introduced the telegraph and postal systems, constructed more canals and bridges, and oversaw the expansion of the cotton industry—which had been initiated under Muhammad Ali—which flourished as a result of the American Civil War, which prevented southern cotton production from reaching the world market.

The British Occupation, 1892–1947

Ismail's expansion caused Egypt to be in heavy international debt. This weakened the nation and left it open for more British intervention. An economic crisis caused the khedive to abdicate in 1879 and the British waited in the wings. It would not be long before their time would come to run the country. But in the meantime, Ismail's son, Tewfik Pasha, would run the country as a transition figure.

Tewfik Pasha wanted to reform the country's economy, and soon gave over the financial management of the nation to Britain. Nationalists, disappointed that Tewfik would hand over the control of the nation's finances to a Christian nation, forced him to appoint their leader Ahmed Orabi as Minister of War. The European reaction to this move on the part of the nationalists was swift, brutal, and decisive. They defeated Orabi's army at Tel El Kabir and shelled both Alexandria and Ismailia. Tewfik was subsequently nothing more than a British puppet. Orabi was exiled and Mustafa Kamil became the leader of the nationalist movement.

The British wasted no time in turning Egypt into a bona fide colony. Egypt was made dependent on British imported goods, and Egyptian cotton was exported to the industrialized European nations as raw material. Egyptian people were once again made the victims of an outside people.

When World War I broke out, Egypt was made formally a part of the British Empire. The Ottoman sultan declared his support for the German government, and this effectively ended any legal authority that the Ottomans had over Egypt. It was now a British subject because England was at war with Germany and its allies. During World I, Fouad I, the sixth son of

Khedive Ismail, was made Khedive of Egypt. His authority was constantly challenged by Egyptian nationalists who used the popular resentment of foreign domination as their main issue.

When Sa'ad Zaghlul became the leader of the nationalist movement in 1918, he presented the British with a demand for complete autonomy for Egypt. It was rejected out of hand. Zaghlul was arrested, tried, and deported to Malta. This led to scores of anti-British riots. The British were forced to back down on Zaghlul's persecution. By 1922 the British were willing to end the protectorate and recognize Egypt's independence, however, they insisted on maintaining control over essential government institutions and the Suez Canal. This allowed the British to effectively control the activities of the Egyptian people. Since economic control was in the hands of the British, all political decisions had to be submitted to the British for approval. In fact, Fouad I was made King of Egypt in March 1922 with the permission of the British. But this was to prove a difficult and troublesome decision. The British were active in trying to enlist intellectuals to support the decision and some of them did. Others initially agreed to the choice and then decided to chart independent pathways. Such may have been the case of Ahmad Amin.

Amin was born in 1886 and died in 1954. As one of the leading political thinkers during Egypt's quest for a popular government, Ahmad Amin's intellectual ideas had a great influence on the nature of Egyptian parliamentary democracy. A student of Egypt's struggle for political freedom is forced, in many ways, to deal with the writings of Ahmad Amin whose career may be said to embody all of the contradictions of Egyptian society.

Amin's liberal credentials and beliefs in democracy were well-known during his life, yet he often doubted that the masses of people in Egypt could be left to their own judgment about political matters. His concept of political governance was intensely moralistic and directed. Amin both influenced and was influenced by his times. He was the son of a well-respected sheikh of the al-Azhar community, and his early childhood education was quite traditional and religious. But during his early manhood he began to sympathize with the views of many Western intellectuals and soon transferred his allegiance from the traditional values of Egypt to those of the westernizing segment of society.

When Ahmad Amin went to study and then to teach at the school for *shari'a* (Muslim law) judges, he tried to introduce to the future leaders ideas of the Western thinkers along with those of traditional Islamic thinkers. The ethical and social thought of modern Europe was a key factor in his development, and he kept close contact with fellow teachers who had studied in England or France. Amin would not visit Europe until he was well past forty years of age. By 1926 he had made his transition to the Westernizing cadre of intellectuals in Cairo. Largely at the suggestion of the immensely influential Taha Hussein, he accepted a teaching job at the University of Cairo that, at the time, was called the Egyptian University. He taught Arabic and Islamic literature there until he retired in 1946.

Amin became one of the most active Egyptian intellectuals, a sort of old man of letters, until his death in 1954. From the time of his retirement in 1946 until his death, he was actively involved in writing and editing for the magazines and journals that were having an impact on Egyptian life. He was the elder statesman of intellectuals, having written an influential and popular history of the first four centuries of Islamic culture. He also engaged in submitting short essays and articles to the popular periodicals such as *al-Hilal* and the literary magazine *al-Risala*.

One can gather something of Amin's thought by examining his opinions on various topics. One of the most telling liberal positions in the writings of Amin is his belief in the right of unpopular opinions to be presented. But he is also a student of parliamentary-style democracy and believes that the institutions of such a democracy must be preserved. When Taha Hussein was dismissed from the university in 1931, Ahmad Amin supported him in the writing of a book on pre-Islamic poetry. Tremendous conservative pressure was brought to bear on the university to replace Hussein for not bowing to the dictates of the government leaders. Already by the early 1930s Amin had found his way to the liberal side of the issues. He did not want to see politics meddling in literature. He was fearful that should Egypt give up its monarchy it would have a government that was republic in name only and based in reality in tyranny and suppression of freedom of speech.

Although recognizing all of the components of liberal democracy and giving lip service to them, Amin's contradiction seemed to be in the fact that he could hardly envision a world in which the majority of the people would be given complete reign over the government. In that sense, he wanted to support the monarchy but not a monarchy beholden to an outside power. Political leadership, according to Amin, must know the correct goals and lead the people toward those goals. But neither Amin nor any other nationalist leader, Western-oriented or otherwise, could prevent Britain from making its tragic and historic decision to back Fouad I.

A power struggle ensued between the people, the king, and the British in the years that followed the coronation of Fouad I. The Wafd Party had the support of the population and took the leadership in campaigning for more rights and freedoms. Having campaigned among the poor masses of Cairo and other regions of the country, the Wafd Party—founded by Sa'ad Zaghlul and led by the autocratic Mustafa an-Nahhas Pasha—had succeeded in amassing a large following among the ordinary Egyptians.

When Farouk I, the son of Fouad I, ascended the throne, he was greeted with some enthusiasm because the people were impressed that he was the first ruler, and the only descendant of the Albanian dynasty of Muhammad Ali Pasha to speak fluent Arabic. Prior to King Farouk I, the other leaders had used Turkish as the court language. In addition, the population believed that Farouk I, had nationalist sympathies and wanted to show their support for a king who believed in the rights of the people. He could not, however, defy the British. His weakness was soon evident, and the young king signed an agreement with the British, called the Anglo–Egyptian Treaty (1936), which ostensibly ended the British occupation but gave them the right to remain in the Suez Canal.

At the outbreak of World War II, the Wafd Party supported the Allies with the understanding that when the war was over, Egypt would gain full independence. However, hatred of the British inspired members of the clandestine al-Ikhwan al-Muslimin (Muslim Brotherhood) to throw their support to the Germans. Therefore, Egypt was thrust into the forefront of the war, becoming a major strategic base of operations during World War II. Cairo and Alexandria were overrun with soldiers, political exiles, spies, and diplomats. The decisive battle at El-Alamein (November 1942) in the desert outside of Alexandria defined the North African Campaign. General Bernard Montgomery's Eighth Army drove back General Field Marshal Erwin Rommel's Afrika Korps and the Allies claimed all of North Africa as the prize.

The defeat of Germany in North Africa was to be the beginning of the end for the Muhammad Ali dynasty supported by the British government. King Farouk I, a descendant of the Albanian Ali, was considered popular, but inherent in his rule were the festering problems of running a monarchy out of touch with the real issues of the people. Farouk I was known to be uneducated, but with a quick charm and an easy manner, but he would not be the person to lead Egypt to independence. Indeed, he had a weakness for surrounding himself with correct advisers and those who flattered him, even in his ignorance. By the late 1940s, there were rumors of scandals in his private life. Britain sought to use him, but in its support of him it was also trapped. Thus, there was a corrupt monarchy and a corrupt occupation. Both the king and the occupiers had to leave in order for freedom to come to Egypt.

At this time, political discontent was surfacing in Egypt. It would soon boil over and leave the country without a king or an occupier, but, instead, with a new leader. The players were the Wafd Party and the Muslim Brotherhood, which was founded by Hasan al-Banna, a brilliant organizer and preacher. He created national consciousness by setting up cells, battalions, youth groups, and a secret apparatus. Al-Banna declared to the al-Ikhwan, "You are not a benevolent society, nor a political party, nor a local organization having limited purposes. Rather, you are a new soul in the heart of the nation to give it life by means of the Qur'an" (Hopwood 1982, 21).

Islam was the totality of everything. There would be no society, no politics, no institutions without it. The al-Ikhwan allowed no such distinctions. To further their aims, the brotherhood used infiltration, propaganda, organization, and intimidation. They rationalized the inherent threats in their militancy by the concept of *jihad* (struggle against those who did not believe in Islam). They did not shirk from death or martyrdom if they felt that it was for the cause of Islam. By the time they reached their peak in the early 1950s, they had more than two thousand branches and half a million members.

Alongside the al-Ikhwan was an activist group called the "Misr al-Fatah" (Young Egypt), a conservative, right-wing organization that was founded by Ahmad Husain in 1933 and became a political party in 1938. The organization created a paramilitary organization called the "Green Shirts" that had as its purpose the purging of the society of Communists, European influences, and foreign privileges. In regard to its battle against the foreign influences in the society, the Misr al-Fatah was similar to the al-Ikhwan. They both were ardently against the British occupation and held a belief in the role of Egypt as the leader of the Islamic world.

Students in the society were often divided between the Wafd and the al-Ikhwan, with the Communists joining the Wafd and the Misr al-Fatah joining the al-Ikhwan. Each organization sought to enlist students in their drive to create a revolutionary spirit. There is little wonder why, between 1945 and 1952, the Egyptian society was on the verge of explosion. The country lived in terror. Speech was restricted and the press was prohibited from printing certain stories. In addition to all of the political troubles, a terrible cholera epidemic struck the nation during the time that it was discovering international isolation. The internal pressures of political agitation, student unrest, social disturbances, terrorism, and threats would eventually lead to a new society. But it would come about not so much because of the al-Ikhwan, Misr al-Fatah, or their allies, but because of a select, secretive group of army officers calling themselves "Free Officers Committee."

The Wafd Party called for the immediate independence of Egypt with the Allies' victory in the war. The party also called for British troops to evacuate Egyptian soil. The British did not respond to this demand with any speed, and thus, Egyptian resentment exploded into anti-British riots and strikes.

The Muslim Brotherhood instigated protests that made the British gover-nance quite difficult because al-Banna had built the brotherhood into a mighty force during the war years.

The Muslim Brotherhood had taken a political stand on the war that said it was not about Muslims or Egypt but about Europeans and their at-tempt to divide up the world. The brotherhood did not openly oppose Egyptian support for the Allies during the war but actively agitated against the British after the war. Pressure from the Wafd Party and the Muslim Brotherhood finally forced the British out of Alexandria and the Canal Zone in 1947.

Israel was established in 1948, and the Arab nations invaded the same year to protect the Arab people of Palestine and to defeat the newly created gov-ernment of the Jewish state. But the smaller state of Israel defeated the Arab forces and created a serious political situation in Egypt. A group of young and idealistic leaders of the army prepared to take the reins of government and assert Egyptian dignity.

Parliamentary elections were held in 1952, and the Wafd Party won the majority of the seats. Mustafa an-Nahhas Pasha was made prime minister. One of the first things he did was to repeal the 1936 Anglo–Egyptian Treaty, which gave Britain the right to remain at the Suez. King Farouk I dismissed the prime minister, and the country erupted in rebellions that had to be put down by force. It was this event that led the Free Officers Committee to stage a coup d'etat. They seized control of the government and forced King Farouk I to abdicate. General Naguib, as the senior officer, became prime minister and commander of the armed forces.

However, the real power was the nine-man Revolutionary Command Council (RCC) under the leadership of Colonel Gamal Abdel Nasser. The RCC ruled decisively. In many respects it had hundreds of years of built-up resentment on its side as it cleared the way for a new regime in Egypt. It abolished the monarchy and all political parties, including the Wafd Party. A year later the RCC declared the Egyptian Arab Republic.

As the RCC became increasingly more radical, it offended the older Na-guib who tried to place some controls over the younger officers. There was a sense that Naguib retained too much of the old traditions to be useful in advancing the rights of Egyptians. There was dissatisfaction with him, and the bickering in the ranks of the junior officers, those who had risked every-thing to bring about change, would lead to distrust of Naguib. Soon Naguib was placed under house arrest and removed from power in 1954. Nasser was made acting head of state, and in 1956 officially assumed the presidency of the republic.

The Era of Gamal Abdel Nasser, 1952–1970

Gamal Abdel Nasser was a dynamic leader who left an indelible mark on the Egyptian and Arab peoples. He transformed the way the Egyptian nation viewed itself and attempted to mold the nation as both an African nation and an Arab nation. He joined the Organization of African Unity and helped to found the Organization of Arab Unity. Both organizations—one geographic and the other cultural—were to play a role in the emerging Egyptian ethos.

Nasser was a charismatic patriot, but ultimately during his leadership, he imposed a socialist-style dictatorship on the country in an attempt to stifle unrest and protest. Inevitably, opposition leaders were jailed, persecuted, tortured, or executed. Nasser sought to make his governance easier by getting rid of all opposing parties. The now-powerful Muslim Brotherhood was outlawed and its members imprisoned although it had been one of the most important supporters of the 1952 revolution. Journalists who disagreed with Nasser's policies were imprisoned. The Wafd Party, which had been abolished, tried to reinvent itself, and was immediately outlawed. All the time this was happening, Nasser achieved unprecedented popularity in the Arab world.

There were several concrete reasons for his popularity. He was the first openly Arab leader, in hundreds of years in Egypt. The country had seen a procession of non-African and non-Arab leaders, and the rise of Nasser, as an Arab nationalist committed to uplifting the rural poor, reverberated throughout the land. He sought to improve the lot of the masses of peasants who farmed the banks of the Nile River. He called for pan-Arab unity in an effort to bring coordinated responses to regional crises. His drive for a pan-Arabism included recognizing the various colors of Arab peoples. Thus, many blacks participated in Nasser's revolution as Arabs. Furthermore, he dramatically nationalized the Suez Canal and stood against British invasion of Egyptian territory. His outspoken criticism of Israel brought about the wrath of the Western world, but Egypt then found assistance from the Soviet Union. But his popularity was matched on the other side by intense dislike by his enemies. They saw him as one who would disturb the vested interests of hundreds of years of power, and thus, he had strong opposition. There was both fervent adulation and intense hostility toward Nasser.

However, he saw himself as a unifier against Western imperialism, and when he was proclaimed prime minister of the new republic in 1954, he consolidated his policies against foreign intervention. One of his first acts was the removal of British troops from the Suez Canal zone. He subsequently deported thousands of Egypt's foreign residents and confiscated their property stating that it had been gained on the backs of the Egyptian people.

What Nasser explained to the people was that in order to build a "democratic, socialist and cooperative society" it was necessary to remove those who were seen as taking wealth without giving back to the society. Thus, he instituted land reforms and redistribution and expanded education. By 1956 he had become president of Egypt.

Nasser established an alliance with Syria as a display of pan-Arabism. This attempt to form a united country of Egypt and Syria was doomed from the beginning because the two countries had two different histories and different customs. In addition, it turned out that Nasser was more of an Egyptian nationalist than a pan-Arabist.

Moving to enhance his international credentials, Nasser helped form the Non-aligned Movement. Alongside India's Jawaharlal Nehru, Ghana's Kwame Nkrumah, Yugoslavia's Josip Broz Tito, and Indonesia's Sukarno, Nasser was a major influence in charting the course between the West and the East. He became a power broker in the developing world. But his internationalism helped to create an image of Egypt as a nation on the move. When the United States and the Western nations refused to grant him funds to build the Aswan High Dam, Nasser turned to the Soviet Union. The dam was a major success in transforming Egypt's agricultural development by preventing the annual flooding that washed away millions of acres of farms. It also added about 15 percent more arable land to the nation.

The Six Day War in 1967 shattered Nasser's pan-Arab dream. Defeat by Israel meant that the Arab nations had suffered a humiliation, and Nasser, as the most outspoken Arab leader, had lost his political edge. His rhetoric was like hot air. The defeat of the Egyptian army and the loss of the Sinai were great blows to the prestige of the country.

Nasser offered to resign, but the people, out of respect for him, staged massive demonstrations to encourage him to remain in office. He did stay in office and ruled until he died of a heart attack on September 1, 1970. As a leader, he had built a personal machine, a political culture dedicated to his vision, and dependent on his leadership. This personalized leadership style meant that all policies stemmed from the presidency. He was motivated by a deep love for Egypt and a real concern for the welfare of the people. It is likely that his regime was able to sustain itself through many crises because of the strong belief the people had in Nasser. After serving for nearly eighteen years as the central figure in the revolution, Nasser's death left a major gap in the political life of the nation.

The Rule of Anwar Sadat, 1970–1981

Anwar Sadat was one of the original members of the Free Officers Committee who led the revolution in 1952. He served as a rather undistinguished vice president to Gamal Abdel Nasser. However, when he assumed the presidency, he immediately began to dismantle many of the harsh policies of his predecessor. In fact, he expelled the Soviet technicians that had been brought into the country by Nasser when the Aswan High Dam was being built. Like Nasser's expulsion of foreign residents, Sadat's expulsion of Soviet citizens in July 1972 was also popular with the masses, but it created international turmoil in the context of the Cold War between the United States and the Soviet Union.

Under Sadat's leadership there were many domestic and foreign policy changes. He sought to keep liberalization of the internal society as a priority by increasing education, speaking out for women's rights, and curtailing the secret police. He demanded that the confiscation of private property be stopped and gave more freedom to the press.

Sadat proved to be an able leader. Perhaps the action that made him a hero to the Egyptian people was the surprise attack on the Israeli forces in the Sinai on the Jewish holiday of Yom Kippur during the Muslim holy month of Ramadan on October 6, 1973. This gave Sadat credibility and he earned the respect of his countrymen. The October War destroyed the idea of Israeli invincibility that had grown from the Six Day War. In the end, the war was fought to a stalemate, but Sadat still emerged a hero.

Moves were made to liberalize the government and the Egyptian system. Many political prisoners were given amnesty, the press was allowed to publish with more freedom, and political parties were allowed. Another action that instilled a sense of pride in the Egyptian people was that Sadat was a devout Islamist. He reversed the secularism that was imposed as a socialist solution and aligned himself with the traditionally religious middle classes. Establishing a policy he called *Infitah* ("Open Door"), Sadat encouraged foreign investments and the development of the private sector. Arab oil money began to flow into the country and foreign aid increased as the nation saw an outbreak of democracy.

Sadat became an increasingly skillful politician and international personality. He was known for dramatic actions. When the International Monetary Fund (IMF) put pressure on the country to stop granting food subsidies because they were draining the country's financial reserves, Sadat responded by stopping the subsidies in one day rather than in a gradual manner. Food prices doubled in one day, which led to massive riots, called "food riots," and forced the United States to increase foreign aid as well as forced the IMF to back down from its call for the end to subsidies. The debt of the country was rescheduled, and Sadat immediately reinstalled the subsidies.

The most dramatic move made by Sadat occurred on November 19, 1977, when he suddenly traveled to Jerusalem with overtures of peace between Egypt and Israel. This was considered a brilliant diplomatic stroke and it placed Sadat and Egypt in the international spotlight and put pressure on Israel. His daring made him a highly respected leader in the West as well as the Arab champion of diplomacy. He gave the Egyptians an image of courage and valor to the European and American peoples.

One of the high points in modern Egyptian diplomacy occurred when Sadat took the initiative to go to Israel and meet with the leaders of that country. It has been recorded in various history books that the bold diplomatic action by Sadat was one of the major political moves in history. At a time when no one expected any Arab-dominated nation to offer a hand to Israel for negotiation, Sadat struck a magnanimous chord in the hearts of the world's peoples by demonstrating his willingness to trust.

The meeting with Prime Minister Menachem Begin and the Israeli Knesset was historic for many reasons, but the overriding issue was Sadat's ability to believe that the Israelis were interested in making peace, not war. He had shown himself a warrior, and now he was showing himself a peacemaker. However, there was trouble on the homefront. Some Arabs believed that he had betrayed their traditional hostility toward Israel and the West and had reduced Egypt to a puppet of the West. Sadat did not like these references nor did he really deserve them since his only crime was trying to bring peace to the region. Nevertheless, those who had welcomed his initiatives at first now felt that he had sold out to the West. Economic liberalization meant that the rich got richer and the poor got poorer because those who had international contacts could do business where those who did not have such contacts were left to their own devices. The Arab League moved its office from Cairo to Tunis as a protest against Sadat's role in the Camp David Accords. Egypt had become the first Arab nation to recognize Israel, and for this action Sadat and Menachem Begin received the Nobel Peace Prize. But the action isolated Sadat from many other Arab leaders.

The groups that Sadat had defended and supported by "un-banning" them, such as the Muslim Brotherhood and the Wafd Party, began to criticize him. Some called him a sellout to Zionist interests. Others called for his assassination. The Western media also criticized him because he tried to repress the Egyptians who were now calling for his assassination. In the end, Sadat was left with few major supporters in the region. In October 1981 while watching a military parade, he was shot and killed. The nation mourned but there was none of the passionate outpouring for him as there had been at the death of Nasser. Yet history has been quite kind to Anwar Sadat, casting him in the role of the wise elder brother who understood inherently what was needed to move the impasse in the negotiations with

Israel and acted to capture the moment in a decisive fashion, carving out for himself a unique persona.

The Time of Hosni Muhammad Mubarak, 1981–Present

Hosni Muhammad Mubarak served as vice president under Anwar Sadat from 1974 until his own ascendancy to the presidency on October 13, 1981. He has served as head of state longer than either Nasser or Sadat. Mubarak was born in 1928 to an upper-middle-class family and has a military education. In Egypt, he attended the National Military Academy and the Air Force Academy, and in the Soviet Union, he studied at the Frunze General Staff Academy.

During the time of Nasser and Sadat, he was a rather low-key military personality. He joined the Egyptian Air Force in 1950 and it was nineteen years later that he was elevated to the rank of Air Force Chief of Staff. He served in that capacity until 1972 when he was made Commander in Chief. In addition to that post he was the Deputy Minister of War and one of Sadat's closest military advisers. He was much like Sadat, a man of ordinary ambition and personality, without charismatic oratory or dramatic flair, before becoming president. However, since ascending to the presidency, Mubarak has continued the more popular policies of Sadat. He has consciously paid more attention to the daily administration of the country and had shown little inclination for thrusting himself into the forefront of Arab politics until the 1990s. He has been concerned with the technological and industrial development of Egypt more than with establishing a strong international presence. As president of Egypt, Mubarak is accepted by some Arabs as the natural leader of the Arab world because he is the leader of the largest and most important state in the Arab world.

It should be pointed out that Hosni Mubarak took over Egypt in an orderly succession when Sadat was assassinated. He was later approved overwhelmingly in a referendum. Given his attempt to follow some of the more liberal policies of Sadat, Mubarak has tried to suppress the fundamentalism that frequently threatens the economy and the stability of the Egyptian society. His program has been one of economic reforms, the increase of political freedom, the expansion of the rights of women, the acceptance of the Muslim Brotherhood into the parliament, and more freedom for the press. Internationally, Mubarak has tried to be neutral between the great powers and has sought to improve relationships between Arab nations. He was reelected in 1987 with 97 percent of the votes in an election with no opposing candidates.

Mubarak has achieved his stature by resuming diplomatic relationships with Arab nations that had broken off relations when Sadat recognized Israel, showing openness toward the Palestinians, and supporting journalistic opinions and freedoms. At the beginning of the 1990s, Egypt was again playing a major role in regional politics. Under Mubarak, in 1990, Egypt supported Kuwait and Saudi Arabia against Iraq in the Gulf War. Later, Egypt sent 38,500 troops to join with the United States and an international force to defeat the armies of Iraq and force them to leave Kuwait.

Despite the keen insights and deft political moves of Mubarak, the country has many problems owing to its long and complex political history and explosive population growth. Egypt is one of the fastest-growing countries in Africa, and the social services have not been able to keep up with the increase in population. Cairo alone has 20 million people. It is one of the five largest cities in the world in terms of population.

Tourism has become one of the biggest foreign exchange earners for the country, but Islamic fundamentalists have frequently disrupted the tourist trade with violent actions. Mubarak has insisted that the nation needs the foreign currency that comes from the tourists. He has enhanced the security measures around the major tourist attractions to keep the tourists safe. Terrorism against foreigners is meant as a protest against Mubarak and is a way to damage the government. In 1994, the government was able to break the back of the terrorist group, called Al-Saeed, in Upper Egypt, and there was a revival of Saudi and Gulf State tourism. Nevertheless, the Mubarak government has had to be vigilant to maintain domestic peace. Many programs to increase the living standards of the peasants have been introduced.

President Hosni Mubarak was reelected in 1993 for a third term; and then on September 26, 1999, he was reelected for an unprecedented fourth six-year presidential term. He won nearly 94 percent of the votes in a popular referendum. Assuming the role of a senior statesman, he was actively involved in the negotiations between Israel and the Palestinians, serving as a confidant, prodder, and mediator. This position placed Egypt squarely on the stage of the largest political drama of the North Africa–Southwest Asia (NASA) region of the world. Mubarak has been eager to position Egypt to become a major player in the political evolution of the region. In fact, Egypt's outlook to the rest of Africa has been one of rivalry in the north with Libya, a country that has clearly focused on the rest of the continent of Africa as its natural economic and political partner. Egypt is a member of the COMESA (Common Market for Eastern and Southern Africa) and has worked to bring about free trade in Africa. In the past, Egypt has been tightly tied to the destiny of Sudan; in fact, many Egyptians see Sudan as an organic part of its own Nile Valley. The two countries—Egypt and Sudan—have been united in the past as one country, and under Mubarak, Egypt takes an interest in the political developments of the country. The role of Egypt in the Arab world has been important since the days of the Muslim Arab conquest under General El As in 639 C.E. With its focus on solidifying its cultural and political leadership in northeast Africa and the Arab world, Egypt remains the dominant player in the region (*Emerging Egypt* 2001, 12).

One of the complaints often heard by those who do not like the slow pace of democracy in Egypt is that Mubarak is "too cautious." In fact, Hala Mostapha was quoted as saying, "He is obsessed with stability" (*Time Europe*, November 27, 2000, Vol. 156, no. 22). The truth of the matter is that Mubarak recognizes the dangers to his economy and society should the militant Islamists want to create havoc. He is sure that the masses of the people will suffer; therefore, he keeps a steady hand on the Egyptian ship of state. In fact, the September 11, 2001, terrorist attacks on the Pentagon and the World Trade Center in the United States sent shock waves through the Egyptian economy. In many ways, because Egypt is the largest economy in northern Africa and southwest Asia in addition to being the most important Muslim country in that part of the world, it is also very susceptible to hostilities involving the West. When it was discovered that the Egyptian Jihad might be connected to the Al-Qaeda organization, many American and European tourists cancelled their visits to Egypt, causing business earnings to plummet, with the ripple effect being felt in subsidiary industries. Thus, the aim of Mubarak has been to bring his country into a more democratic era in which the presence of different religions would not necessarily create hostility. The emergence of Mubarak's son Gamal as a leader of the National Democratic Party (NDP) will bring some new life into the political party and position the party for future elections. Gamal, who is thirty-nine, might even be a potential successor to his father.

There are many issues, however, that must be confronted before Egypt is truly stabilized. Yet the stability that exists at the present time is the best that has existed since the revolution of 1952. The country under Mubarak is at peace with all of its neighbors and has become one of the anchors in the political and economic community of the region. Because of the strength of Mubarak's policies, his relationship with the Saudis, his ability to handle the United States, and his deftness in dealing with the Palestinian question, Egypt has the respect of its neighbors and has become the leading actor in the regional drama.

The two remaining issues that must be dealt with are the Palestinians and the fundamentalists. One is an international political issue and the other is a domestic issue. The government of Mubarak has tried to defend Arab rights while being a moderator in the region. Diplomatically, Egypt defined its role in 2000 as the "nursemaid of the peace process" between the Arabs and Israelis. President Mubarak has backed Palestinian Authority President Yasser

Arafat publicly and the two consult privately. In this way, Arafat has received moral and economic support from Egypt. Mubarak has encouraged Arafat to stand firm on his principles of human rights and justice, yet he encourages him to make concessions when necessary to make the Israelis feel safe. The Palestinian problem is Mubarak's greatest challenge and it became increasingly difficult after the September 11, 2001, terrorist bombings.

Leading other Arab heads of state as the voice of moderation, President Mubarak has created a role for his country in the Israeli–Palestinian conflict. His mediation was credited with restarting negotiations after the suspension of talks due to the *intifada*, a period of Palestinian uprising in 1996–1999. The diplomatic prestige of Egypt has grown under Mubarak to the point where he is listened to and consulted by all of the major Western governments before they act in the region. The Egyptian government gets more than $2 billion in aid annually from the United States. It is often said that the money is in exchange for Egypt being the first state in the region to make peace with Israel. No one in the Western world wants Egypt's economy to collapse because of the danger this would bring to the region.

President Mubarak has visited Washington once a year for the past five years. He is seeking to ready his country for the time when the overall American aid will be cut to $400 million. A number of issues have emerged over the last few years between the United States and Egypt, but none have derailed the relationship between the two nations. One issue that threatened to create problems for the relationship was the crash of Egypt Air's Flight 990 from New York to Cairo in October 1999. American investigators concluded that the copilot, Gamil al-Batouty, may have deliberately crashed the plane. A flood of protest from the Egyptian government caused this issue to be minimized in the American press. Mubarak is credited with convincing the Americans to downplay the possibility of a suicide on the part of al-Batouty.

On the domestic front, President Mubarak has been able to subdue the al-Ikhwan al-Muslimin and other groups with strong police pressure to ensure a stable society. Politically, he has been able to convert many opposition leaders to his form of government or, at least, align them with his policies. Only the radical fundamentalists remain outside of the Pax Mubarak. When one thinks of the fact that President Mubarak achieved limited agricultural reform and privatization without an explosion of unrest among the peasants it is almost miraculous. His low-key approach to the political process—not too much rhetoric and flamboyance—has played exceptionally well in moderating the influences in Egypt that could have caused trouble.

The World Trade Center and Pentagon attacks in New York and Washington made an Egyptian, Ayman al-Jawahiri (an associate of Osama bin

Laden), of the Islamic Jihad a household name. It is believed that al-Jawahiri's organization was closely related to the Al-Qaeda organization of Osama bin Laden.

NOTES

1. For a long time it was assumed that the term "Ta-wy" referred to the concepts of "red" and "black" land; however recent scholarship has taken this term to mean "desert" and "fertile." This seems more likely since the earth in Egypt is often red or brown, but the vegetation along the river banks is green and verdant. At one time, perhaps, it may have been easy to argue the "black" soil thesis, but there is no reason to do so now.

2. Egypt asserts rights to the Hala'ib Triangle, a barren area of 7,946 square miles under partial Sudanese administration that is defined by a boundary that supersedes the treaty boundary of 1899.

3. All three of the Nubian groups—Kanuz, Mahas, and Matoki—are usually referred to by the general name "Nubi" although they have distinct languages.

2

Government, Economy, Education, and Tourism

THE CIVIL GOVERNMENT

THE EGYPTION NATION is divided into three branches: the executive, the legislative, and the judiciary. Egypt is a democratic country. Of the more than 4,000 candidates running for election during 1999 in Egypt, 444 were members of the ruling National Democratic Party (NDP), 428 were from the opposition, and the remainder were independents. There is some belief that should the opposition increase its proportion of representation in the parliament through persuasion or the fracture of the NDP, the country could be a republican version of Morocco or Jordan, "where an on-partisan head of state presides over a pluralistic parliament" (*Emerging Egypt* 2001, 17).

The president of the nation is the head of state and the leader of the executive branch. Normally, the nomination of the president is made by the National Assembly and the candidate who receives two-thirds of the votes of the members is referred to the nation for a plebiscite. Hosni Mubarak has been overwhelmingly elected to the presidency in the last two elections. However, the opposition parties have made inroads at all levels of the government.

The government is the supreme executive and administrative instrument of the state. It is made up of the prime minister and the assembly members, some of whom may be members of the legislature. The president appoints and removes governors.

Judicial supervision of the 2000 election in Egypt was supposed to assure the nation of a fair process. However, the poll was marred by some incidences of violence. Armed groups prevented some voters from enjoying the privilege of voting in some sections of the country. Battles with some security forces occurred in the working-class neighborhood of Shubrâ el-Kheima. The election resulted in more opposition party members being elected, particularly the Islamists. Their eighteen seats were won when the Muslim Brotherhood placed intense pressure on some voters. On the left, the Tagammu Party, the Democratic Nasserist Party, and independent Nasserists, won thirteen seats.

The judiciary is independent as are the judges, and in the matter of their deliberations, opinions, and experience, they are subject to no other authority except the law. The ultimate law in Egypt is Islamic law. In every respect, Egypt is a nation of law and civic responsibility.

The national anthem of Egypt "My Homeland" avoids any statement of religion; instead, it concentrates on duty to homeland and mentions the Nile and its gifts to humanity in a grand gesture of national nobility:

> My homeland, my homeland, my hallowed land,
> Only to you, is my due hearty love at command,
> My homeland, my homeland, my hallowed land,
> Only to you is my due hearty love at command,
> Mother of the great ancient land,
> My sacred wish and holy demand,
> All should love, awe and cherish thee,
> Gracious is thy Nile to humanity,
> No evil hand can harm or do you wrong,
> So long as your free sons are strong,
> My homeland, my homeland, my hallowed land,
> Only to you, is my due hearty love at command.

The first national flag was established by a royal decree in 1923 when Egypt gained conditional independence from Great Britain in 1922. In 1958, a presidential decree established a new flag for the United Arab Republic, which comprised a merger of Syria and Egypt. In 1972, a new law changed the style of the flag and added a golden hawk to replace the stars; and finally in 1984, the current flag was created replacing the hawk with a golden eagle representing the eagle of Saladin of the Crusades.

Modern Egypt is divided into fourteen regions. Each region has a governor. The major regions have as capitals the principal cities of Egypt. Ancient Egypt had forty-two nomes or provinces, however, since the times of the pharaohs, Egypt has undergone many administrative changes reflecting the wishes of the governing authorities. The present fourteen regions appear to be easily governed under the current political climate.

Fertile lands irrigated from the Nile River

ECONOMY

Like other modern economies, Egypt is not without its problems and issues. In discussing the modern developments in the society, it is useful to remember that water, urbanization, relocation of minority populations, the Aswan High Dam, tourism, and politics continue to define the quality of Egyptian life. To understand how these issues have played out and are playing out in the contemporary society, it is necessary to present some general details.

The Nile River

The Nile River has been one of the two important factors in Egyptian history from time immemorial, but during the past forty years, human attempts to control the river have produced numerous advantages and disadvantages that will have to be confronted in future years. Because of the catastrophic floods that drowned the land annually for thousands of years, the Egyptians have always wanted a way to control the water during the inundation. Several small dams had been built along the river in historic times, but it was the construction of the Aswan High Dam, one of the most difficult and massive public works in history, that would change the way Egypt lived its life along the river.

Agriculture is a major sector of the Egyptian economy. Irrigation is the life blood of agriculture. However, it would take the control of the Nile to bring the most advantageous situation to the farmers. There had been numerous attempts to use the river's water effectively and efficiently prior to the construction of the Aswan High Dam. Actually Nile control works had started in 1843 with the building of El Kanater el Khairiya Barrage at the apex of the Delta with the idea that the water level would be raised upstream and thus enable the water to enter the Delta canals at the low period. The first Aswan dam was built in 1902. That is why the last dam is called the Aswan High Dam. Egypt has more than 24,860 miles of canals and waterworks. Since water is distributed to the various canals according to a rotation system, there are watering and closing days depending on the season and zone. Two systems of drainage occur in Egypt: the first is by free-flow of gravity channels draining toward the sea or lakes, and the second is by lifting the water.

The Aswan High Dam

Egypt seems to demand the monumental. The construction of the Aswan High Dam was one more example of the Egyptian superlative. Building the dam took an enormous amount of resources. The dam was built just north of the Sudanese border near the famous city of Aswan, from which the dam takes its name.

It is a large rock-filled dam that receives the world's longest river and creates the third largest freshwater reservoir in the world—Lake Nasser—named for the first president of the country. The name of the dam in Arabic is Sadd el Aali. It was started in 1952 and it took eighteen years to complete.

Always dependent on the Nile for its livelihood, Egypt was also a victim of the Nile's annual inundation before the building of the Aswan High Dam. The annual floods deposited a million tons of nutrient-rich sediment that helped in agricultural production. This process started millions of years ago, predating the fabled period of the pharaohs. By 1889, the first Aswan dam was built to keep back the floods, but it proved insufficient because the waters of the Nile, coming down from Ethiopia and Uganda, would always overpower the short dam. It was raised in 1912 and then again in 1933 to prevent the water from flooding homes and farms in the rich valley. However, by 1946 the danger to Egypt was revealed when the waters peaked at the top of the dam, even in its extension, and the entire country was fearful.

One of the first major acts of the interim Revolutionary Command Council (RCC) government was to make a decision to build the Aswan High Dam about four miles upstream from the old dam. In 1954, the government of

Egypt requested loans from the World Bank to pay for the cost of the dam, which eventually approached US$1 billion. The U.S. government was one of the first to agree to loan Egypt money for the project but withdrew from the project for political reasons soon after announcing that it would support it. The political reasons given have to do with the Egyptian–Israeli conflict. However, Egypt was not deterred. Two years later the government of President Gamal Abdel Nasser nationalized the Suez Canal to help pay for the construction of the dam. Israel, England, and France invaded Egypt almost immediately and this set up the stage for an East–West conflict over the dam project.

The Soviet Union agreed to help Egypt build the dam, and the offer was accepted. The Soviet Union sent money, technicians, and military advisers to enhance the rapport between the two countries. The project was an awesome and daunting one. To construct the dam, more than 100,000 people who lived above and below the dam had to be relocated. These were mainly Nubians who had lived in the area since time immemorial and had built their temples, erected their tombs, and prayed to their ancestors in the quiet of the desert evenings for thousands of years. They would be uprooted and moved to many villages. The Nubian Egyptians would be moved about thirty miles to the Kom Ombo area. However, the Nubians living in Sudan would have to be moved nearly four hundred miles away from their native lands.

In addition to moving people, the government had to decide what to do about marvelous treasures of art. Do you flood the most sacred temples of the ancient world? What do you do with the Temple of Abu Simbel where Ramses II had built his own tomb and one for his favorite wife, Nefertari? They were also moved.

The dam was one of the most massive projects ever undertaken by humans. The material used in the dam would equal about seventeen of the great pyramids at Giza. Gamal Abdel Nasser died in 1970 knowing that he had left Egypt a great gift for its future. The benefits to Egypt are significant. The dam controls the annual floods and prevents the untold damage that would occur along the floodplain. There are several other benefits; for example the dam keeps the water flow consistent and thereby improves the sailing and navigation.

The dam was constructed to solve one problem but in the process it created another. Seepage and evaporation accounts for about 14 percent loss of the annual input into the reservoir. The second problem is that the sediments of the Nile have been filling the dam, therefore reducing its reservoir and storage capacity. Farmers are now required to use fertilizer to get the same yield as before when the river left nutrient-rich sediment. According to some reports, the shrimp catch in the Mediterranean Sea has become smaller due to the water flow change. Erosion is occurring around the Delta region because there is no additional agglomeration of sediment to keep erosion at bay. Poor drainage of the newly irrigated lands that have appeared along the river has added to the increased salinity of the water. Over one-half of Egypt's farmlands are now rated as having medium to poor soil when once the soil was considered one of the richest in the world.

All is not bad, however, since the lake created by the dam—Lake Nasser—has actually created more land for people to farm on than ever before. This is because of the water stored in the lake, which is used to irrigate the land around it. Lake Nasser has created a huge fishing industry, producing nearly 100,000 tons of fish per year. Thus, the Nile River and the Aswan High Dam are handmaidens of the continuing development of modern Egypt. One could not imagine modern Egypt without the Aswan High Dam or something equivalent to it.

MAJOR CITIES OF EGYPT: URBANIZATION AND THE CONTEMPORARY SOCIETY

Cairo: The Mother of the World

Cairo is one of the world's most exciting cities. It is large, boisterous, and busy, but there are neighborhoods that are quiet and beautiful. The city of Cairo was founded on August 5, 969 C.E. It has become the largest African and Arab city in the world. Outside of its boundaries are the great Giza pyramids, ruins of the ancient city of Memphis (called the "Middle of the Universe"), and the holy city of On (called Heliopolis by the Greeks). It has been written that "Memphis and Heliopolis had been flourishing a thousand years when Alexander visited them; their awe was so potent that the conqueror preferred to build his Egyptian capital not where the pharaohs had reigned but on an island joined to Greece by the sea and separated from Egypt by a lake" (Stewart 1996, 1). But Cairo has not been awed by the illustrious history that surrounds it because the city itself has been the seat of some of the most eventful happenings on the continent of Africa. Furthermore, during the Middle Ages it was the largest city in Africa, and larger than any city in Europe or Asia. Great public buildings were erected by men dedicated to trading between three continents: Africa, Europe, and Asia. Anyone looking to engage in commerce—whether it was gold, incense, or oils—had to come through the merchants of Cairo, that is, until Vasco da Gama, the Portuguese sailor, made it around the cape of Africa in 1498. Europe had discovered that one could reach the East and its rich sources of spice without having to pay Cairo its customary tariffs. Even so, Cairo would

Cairo congestion

continue to exercise its influence in northeast Africa and southwest Asia. This was underscored by the building of the Suez Canal in 1869. Along with the cultivation of cotton, the opening of the Suez made Egypt important and Cairo, as Egypt's capital, became a strategic city in global commerce.

Cairo has played the role of *um al-dunya* ("Mother of the World") in many scenarios in modern times. From its position as the pulse point of the Nile, located at the southern apex of the Delta and the northern point of the valley, Cairo dominates the commerce and wealth of a broad region. It is the guardian of the Egyptian breadbasket, but it is also the greatest inland port on the Nile. Actually, it is well-known that the Nile is an easier river to navigate than the famed Euphrates. Cairo, near the site of the far more ancient city of Memphis that was located on the west bank of the river, was the gateway to the sea—*al-bahr* as the Arabs came to call it.

The Nile flows through the heart of Cairo. In many respects, it is a unique river. One of the most interesting facts about the river is that its dominant winds are from the north to the south, although the most constant tides are from the south to the north. Most major rivers flow southward; but the Nile flows northward. Thus, if a person wanted to travel northward, he or she only had to launch a vessel and be taken by the tides all the way to the Mediterranean. On the other hand, if a person wanted to travel to the south, he or she could simply put up sails and be driven all the way to the sixth

Sailboat (*felucca*) pilot n the Nile

cataract (mistakenly referred to as the first). Of course only since the twentieth century has the Nile been controlled by dams in Upper Egypt. The dams allowed a regulated flow of the waters. If it had not been for the dams the age-long destruction of the houses and farms along the river's banks would have continued. As it is, the people of Egypt knew that their livelihood depended on the good graces of Ethiopia and the Congo area. All Egyptians believed that the waters of the Nile came from "springs in the Mountains of the Moon" (Stewart 1996, 9). Although the Nile was the major avenue for the movement of goods, it was not the only avenue. In fact, caravans across the Eastern Desert and canals over to the Red Sea were often used to transport commerce. They often began and ended in Cairo. As the "Mother of the World" in the minds of its inhabitants, the city was seen as the source of all things good in Egypt. Cairo was the end of the past and the beginning of the future in the minds of those who created it as the cultural center of Egypt.

Cairo was a beacon of light shining from the junction of the narrow Nile Valley with the broad flowing delta region. Situated at the critical point along the Nile River, Cairo became, soon after its founding, the most recognized city in all of Egypt, although it was not the oldest.

One of the great museums in the world is in the heart of Cairo. The Egyptian Museum was founded in 1858 by the Frenchman Auguste-

Entrance to Egyptian Museum of Antiquities

Ferdinand-François Mariette at Bulaq. The present building was erected in 1902. Mariette died in 1881, and his sarcophagus was placed on the west side of the museum's garden in 1904. Egyptology in the nineteenth century accelerated the need for a museum to conserve the findings coming out of Egypt. Although the country lost hundreds of thousands of pieces of ancient works to museums around the world, the Egyptian Museum still retains more than 120,000 pieces, making it the repository of the largest collection of ancient Egyptian works in the world (see also Chapter 4, "Architecture and Art").

Alexandria: The City on the Sea

Alexandria has captured the imaginations of many generations. From the sleepy village of Rakoda (as it was called when Alexander the Macedonian [the Great] founded it) to its glory days as the leading city of the world during the Greek occupation of Egypt, Alexandria has remained Egypt's most outwardly looking city. The Greek architect Dinocrates designed and built the city (332–331 B.C.E.) to immortalize Alexander's name. The city intrigued its earliest visitors, both inviting them and shutting them out at the same time. It was the site of the ancient Lighthouse, one of the Seven Wonders of the Ancient World, as well as the Great Library. Its religious history was ancient and its recent past colorful when the Greeks came to rule.

Alexandria lies northwest of the Nile Delta and stretches along a narrow land strip between the Mediterranean Sea and Lake Mariout. It is linked to Cairo by two major highways and a railroad line. The city is bordered on the east by Abu Qir and on the west by El-Alamein and Sidi Abdul Rahman.

On July 1, 1798, when Napoleon Bonaparte and the French army entered Alexandria, it had a population of less than 10,000. It had once been the second largest city in the world but had shrunk in importance and population by the time the French invaded. Alexandria's population was perhaps centered around an area called Mansheya, a Turkish enclave established when the Ottoman Turks invaded Egypt. The five thousand French soldiers entered the city without opposition in 1798.

Alexandria was at the center of the continuing struggle for external dominance of Egypt. Muhammad Ali, the Albanian appointed as ruler of Egypt by the Ottoman Turks, turned the country into his own private province. In fact, he gave Cleopatra's Needles to the United States and Britain. However, during this period, the British intervened often in Egyptian affairs. Under the successors of Ali, Alexandria continued to grow as a city and by the time of the Suez Canal the city had 94 percent of the country's exports.

In 1882, Ahmed Orabi, an Egyptian nationalist, led a revolt against the Albanian–Turkish dynasty. The British intervened by bombarding Alexandria for two days. The British then occupied the city and set the stage for a seventy-year occupation of the country.

In the twentieth century, the city became Egypt's summer capital, and Al-Montazah Palace was designated as the king's summer residence. It was also the city where the Arab League was born in 1944. By 1952, it was the city that saw the abdication and departure of King Farouk I for exile in Italy.

Contemporary Alexandria is a large city that stretches for forty-five miles along the Mediterranean coast. It is Egypt's most ethnically diverse city with old populations of Greeks, Armenians, Syrians, Jews, Turks, Italians, Maltese, and Lebanese. The city has ethnic neighborhoods with names reflecting the various communities: the Greek names of Bacos (Bacchus) and Quartier Grec (Greek Quarter); Arab names such as Shathy, Sidi Bishr, Sidi Gaher; Jewish names such as Smousha, Menasha; and modern European names such as Fleming Schutz, Stanley, and Lambruco. There is a project underway to revive the old Alexandria library. It will be called Bibliotheca Alexandrina and will be built on the site of the old Caesarium and Ptolemaic Palace.

The city is the home of Alexandria University, the Arab Institute of Science and Technology, Université Senghor, and the Eastern Mediterranean Office of the World Health Organization. This has made it a cosmopolitan center for the eastern Mediterranean area. Today, Alexandria stands as one

Luxor boys

of the most visually attractive cities on the Mediterranean and, with its rich historical background, has become one of the key destinations for Mediterranean travelers.

Luxor

More human monuments are found in and outside of Luxor than any city in the world. It is a city built on tourism, as more and more tourists compete to see the constructions and creations of the ancients. But it is a city of a very modern presence. Served by a major airport and more than five hundred riverboats, Luxor is easily reached and remains one of the principal tourist destinations in the world.

Built on the ancient site of the New Kingdom capital Waset, modern Luxor is the gateway to the memorable temples and tombs of the Valley of the Kings and the Valley of the Queens.

Modern Luxor remains a city of gift shops, hotels, and restaurants, all connected to the historical role the city has played in world history. It is a bustling city with cars, buses, buggies, and taxis racing to take tourists to the various sites.

Tour boat docked at Aswan

Aswan

Aswan is the garden city of Egypt. It is located at the historical border with ancient Nubia. During the Pharaonic Period, when one left Aswan going south one was in the country of the people of Ta-Seti ("Land of the Bow"). Thus, Aswan has a special place in the history of Egypt. It was the source of the Nile in the minds of many Egyptians because of the cataracts in the river, but it was also thought to be the home of the gods. We know, of course, that it was the quarry for the stones that were used to build many of the monuments in lower Kemet. The obelisks erected at Karnak Temple originated in the quarries of Aswan. It was quite common in the ancient period for huge stones to be floated down the river during the inundation. Therefore, Aswan (or Syene, as it was called then) became the center of the stone carvers of ancient Egypt.

Modern Aswan is a bustling city with a lively and dynamic open market, one of the best in Africa. In addition, there are outstanding public buildings, many hotels, and pleasant neighborhoods. The Nubian Museum (opened in 1997) holds one of the largest collections of Nubian art in the world. In fact, it is unrivaled in Egypt in terms of its presentation of art and culture.

THE SUEZ CANAL

Since its creation, the Suez Canal has always been at the center of commerce and politics in Egypt. It has been written that "[i]t gave the British the excuse for staying on until 1955 and for attempting to return in 1956. It was the barrier the Israelis reached in 1956 and 1967 and the waterway across which the war of attrition was fought in 1969" (Hopwood 1982, 133). The Suez is one of the key canals in the world, and thousands of ships pass through it each year.

It would take the Free Officers Committee revolution to change the status of the Suez Canal. In 1952, a board of thirty-two directors controlled the canal. However, only five of those directors were Egyptians. This was one of the complaints of the Egyptian people. The resource, while impacting on the Egyptian people, was in the hands of foreigners. They could not feel a sense of national pride since the canal was effectively in the hands of non-Egyptians. The canal was a thorn in the side of national consciousness. Many people did not want to see Egypt humiliated by allowing all the decisions at the canal to be made by non-Egyptians. In 1956, President Nasser nationalized the canal after finding out that Egypt was only receiving 7 percent of the gross from transit dues. Nasser's announcement that Egypt would receive 100 percent of the transit dues and use the money to build the Aswan High Dam stunned those who believed that Egypt would not be able to run its own affairs. Egypt was dispensing with all aspects of its colonial past, and it did not need to be reminded of it by the canal.

The canal has been run quite efficiently. However, it was closed in 1956 because of the war and again in 1967 due to a war. Egyptians took over the facilities and increased the numbers of transits, improved the operations, and when the Israelis reached the East Bank in June 1967, the canal was blocked. It remained closed to shipping when Nasser died, and it would take President Sadat's resolve to get it reopened. Egypt could not afford to lose the 100 million pounds per year.

The history of the Suez Canal is long. There had been numerous attempts to join the Mediterranean and Red seas since 1887 B.C.E. when Senursert III of the Twelfth Dynasty attempted to dig a canal to make a navigable waterway between the two seas. Psammetichus II, in 609 B.C.E. tried to rejoin the two waterways without success. The Persians also tried it; and then under the Greek king, Ptolemy II, it was reopened and then successively reopened by Trajan and General El As.

The dream of connecting the two waterways without a detour through the Nile, as had been done before, interested a lot of engineers. But the stumbling block seemed to be the idea, from somewhere, that the Mediterranean was 29.5 feet below the level of the Red Sea. This was disproved, and in 1854 a concession was given by Said Pasha to Ferdinand de Lesseps. A company was formed, and on April 22, 1859, work was begun on the Suez Canal. It would take ten years, until November 1869, before it would be finished. When it was finally completed, the canal was 107.5 miles long, 656 feet wide at water level, and its maximum draft for ships would be 37 feet. The speed limit for ships is 12.5 miles per hour.

EDUCATION

In the Western sense, modern education in Egypt probably dates back to the French invasion of 1798–1799. Napoleon's army not only discovered the Rosetta Stone that was later used to break the code of the ancient hieroglyphics, but the Grand Army provided the Egyptian leaders with the opportunity to compare their education with that of the outside world. As one historian noted, "The old culture was subjected to a severe test and in response, Egypt undertook a series of changes to modify its traditional culture" (Faksh 1980, 42). In many ways the Napoleonic charge into the country was a quick wake-up call. The fact of the matter is that Egyptians had been ruled by non-Egyptians for hundreds of years and they were aware of some attitudes of the outside world. What they were not aware of may have been the various ways in which the outside world organized cultural and educational institutions, but this would change.

During the rule of Muhammad Ali (1805–1848), Egypt adopted a new educational system, not to supplant the religious system, but to complement it. This new system was secular, and it rivaled the religious one but did not overtake it. Ali wanted Egypt to partake of the fruits of the international community without losing its own soul by taking the roots of the Western culture.

The old religious system had served the society well at the rudimentary level of providing writing, reading, and arithmetic to a broad section of boys and men. However, the aspiring elite and the ruling politicians wanted more for their children. They sought to introduce a secular system that would allow their children to compete on the international stage. In science and technology and business and art, the new educational elite saw a large opening for secular education.

The modern system has coexisted with the old religious system to the extent that the society bears the marks of the division. There are some who believe that the two systems have prevented national integration and unification. But the dual structure of education has allowed a cultural elite to arise that has an interest in commerce and politics. They represent the eco-

Children singing at school

nomic engine that mobilizes the society. However, the religious system remains attached to the sacred institutions, and the masses of people acquire their knowledge from the religious schools. The religious schools are referred to as the "Azhar System." The Azhar graduates have a different outlook than secular system graduates. Many times they do not agree on the objectives of education. It is claimed that some of those who are trained in the Azhar are usually well versed in the Qur'an but are isolated from the issues of contemporary society. On the other hand the secularly educated often "do not have Arabic fluency and cannot transmit their learning" (Faksh 1980, 43).

The secular schools are dependent on an educated elite. Students are instructed in physics, law, science, and astronomy. They do not have to pay fees. In 1944, fees were abolished in primary schools, and in 1951 they were discontinued at the high school level. However, the expansion of education has been steady during the past thirty years. This has brought more people into the secular system. At one time most of the students who took advantage of the secular system were minorities, such as Copts, Greeks, Jews, Italians, Syrians, and Lebanese.

Egyptian society encourages education. About half of all Egyptians are literate: 63.6 percent of the men and 38.8 percent of the women. In 2001, primary school enrollment approached 100 percent, although only 7.3 percent of the population emerges from the educational system with a college degree (*Emerging Egypt* 2001, 11). There is a belief that education is an integral part of the national life. No nation can actually advance if it does not have a literate public. To appreciate literature you have to be able to read; however, one can appreciate music and art without literacy. Yet literacy is the key to understanding what the major thinkers of a society are saying. Therefore, the government has encouraged education; it has made a special effort to bring the joys of literacy to the rural population. This desire for a literate populace has taken an increasingly larger proportion of the Egyptian budget, but the government has maintained its forward-looking position that education would bring the people greater benefits and more democracy.

Under the Mubarak regime, the government has continued to put emphasis on educating the rural folk. Schools have been built in most of the rural villages and all of the small towns in Upper Egypt. The aim of the government's project in education is to create a safer and more secure environment for political stability and economic prosperity.

TOURISM

Vacation Sites

Egypt has always been a destination for world travelers. The ancient Greek historian Herodotus, one of the first travelers to visit Egypt and to write about his travels, came to the Nile Valley during the fifth century B.C.E. Other people from outside of Africa followed him, but it would be the modern traveler who would discover the great diversity of Egypt's modern contributions. It was the building of the Suez Canal that made Egypt a destination for those interested in modern technology. During the 1960s, the Aswan High Dam would once again thrust Egypt into the forefront as a modern destination of technological prowess. But its record of ancient monuments is impressive, maybe the most impressive of any country in the world.

To cater to the large numbers of visitors, the Egyptian government has encouraged the development of tourist services, including more than five thousand guides, hundreds of tour companies, and scores of hotels. One can discover almost any type of luxury in Egypt from five-star hotels to resort and club hotels on the beaches. Scuba diving in some areas has become a large revenue earner for the economy. But Egypt remains, because of its ancient monumentality, a country sought out by tourists interested in knowing what it was like to live in the world of the pharaohs. Of all the nations in the world Egypt does not disappoint its visitors with its rich and varied history of human activity. Because contemporary Egypt is a modern society

Popular hotel on Elephantine Island

Beautiful grounds of the Mena House Hotel

Modern club and restaurant on the bank of the Nile

with an ancient past, the numerous sites for tourists, both domestic and international, beckon tourists of all economic and social backgrounds.

Nightlife and Entertainment

The major cities of Cairo and Alexandria are among the most open cities in the world in terms of nightclubs. One can usually find several clubs that remain open for most of the night. Typically, Egyptians who venture out at night for entertainment do so at late hours, around ten o'clock in the evening or later. The clubs, therefore, might stay open until five or six in the morning. In Alexandria, the main clubs are the "Crazy Horse," the "Crevette," the "Rokn El-Ferdous," the "Sheraton," the "Dolphin," "Discotheque," and the "Alexandria," among others.

Cairo, of course, has far more clubs than Alexandria because it is, indeed, the "Mother of the World" and people come from all over the Arab and African world to Cairo because of its excitement. One can easily find clubs, restaurants, or cafeterias. There is no reason for the Egyptian to ever feel that he or she does not have anywhere to go or any place to visit. The country even has a number of casinos. But it is the ancient monuments and historical sites that give even contemporary Egypt its special place in the popular imagination (see also Chapter 5, "Social Customs and Lifestyles").

Kiosk of Philae Temple

Ancient Monuments

The ancient monuments of Egypt constitute about one-third of such monuments in the world (see also Chapter 4, "Architecture and Art"). Various movements in Egypt have found the ancient monuments difficult to accept since they existed prior to the development of Islam. During the 1980s, many monuments were attacked as being pagan, heathen, and non-Islamic. Religious zealots saw the historical treasures from the ancient African civilization as contrary to Islam and sought to organize against the preservation of the sites. Fortunately for Egypt and the world, the government has fought against such radical assaults on the great human treasures in the Nile Valley. It has taken its role as the custodian of the monuments with seriousness and has sought to punish those who would destroy the monuments.

Pyramids

There are ninety-six pyramids in Egypt. The Giza plateau has the most spectacular pyramids of which Khufu, Khafre, and Menkaure are among the most beautiful ever built. Giza lies about 6 miles from Cairo.

The most famous structure in the world is the Great Pyramid of Khufu; it was built by Khufu (called Cheops by the Greeks), the second king of the

Statue of Ramses II at Luxor Temple University

Fourth Dynasty. It was erected around 2650 B.C.E. Khufu's pyramid stands 449 feet high (originally it stood at 479 feet). Nearly 2.5 million blocks of stone were used to build the pyramid. It measures 2,743 square feet at its base. What is most astounding about the pyramid is not its size but the precision with which the Egyptians constructed it. On its eastern flank are three small pyramids dedicated to Khufu's wives.

The Pyramid of Khafre was built by Khafre (called Chephren by the Greeks), the second son of Khufu and the fourth king of the Fourth Dynasty. The pyramid is 446 feet high and is located southwest of Khufu. Retaining on its upper parts some of the limestone that had once covered the entire

The Great Sphinx resplendent

pyramid, Khafre gives one a fairly good impression of what it must have looked like with the outside finish on it. It measures 2,312 square feet at its base. The pyramid has two entrances on the north side. Khafre has an accompanying Temple of the Valley, a mortuary temple, where religious rites were performed while embalming the king's body.

A third pyramid, built by Menkaure (called Mycerinus by the Greeks) who was the son of Khafre and the fifth king of the Fourth Dynasty is southwest of Khafre. It is much smaller than the others: 203 feet tall. It is distinguished from the others by the fact that its lower part retains the original granite slab covering. The pyramids were tombs to preserve the bodies of the dead kings who, it was believed, were to experience resurrection and immortality. One can celebrate the brilliant conceptions of the ancient Egyptian people by recognizing that hundreds of tombs dot the landscape of Egypt as a testimony of the people's faith in immortality.

At Giza one can also see the solar boats of Khufu. The wooden boats, meant to be at the disposal of the king when he went on his journey of Day and Night with the Sun God Ra in the afterworld, were discovered on the east and west sides of the Great Pyramid. A huge boat was found behind the great slabs of stone on the south side of the Great Pyramid. It is made of cedar and is in very good condition, the oars, ropes, and a kiosk for sitting were also recovered. The boat, which is now housed in a special museum at the site, is 143 feet long, with a prow of 16 feet and a stern of 23 feet.

Temple at Abu Simbel

Valley of the Kings

Numerous tombs dot the desert landscape of the Valley of the Kings. They represent a veritable history of the New Kingdom and speak to the ingenuity of the ancients in creating enormous monuments to the achievements of the kings and noblemen of the New Kingdom. It was here that the tomb of King Tutankhamen was discovered in 1922. It was also in this valley that the Ramses had their tombs constructed. The valley itself is a graveyard for the most famous names in antiquity.

Temple of Ramses II

One of the greatest wonders of the modern world is an ancient monument on the edge of Lake Nasser at Abu Simbel. The massive temple of Ramses II and the smaller temple of Nefertari, his wife, represent the crowning achievement of construction during the New Kingdom. Here, on what is a barren hilltop, barely six hundred feet from where it was first built, sits one of the treasures of the world. The temple of Ramses II at Abu Simbel has no equal in Egypt and certainly none in any other part of the world.

Historical Christian Sites

Among the Christian sites are the churches located in the old city of Cairo. The principal ones are Al-Mu'allaqah Church (Hanging Church), which dates back to the fourth century; the Church of Abu Sergah; the Church of St. Barbara, founded in the fifth century; the Church of St. Mina, built in the sixth century; the Church of Al-Adra, dating to the eighth century; the Church of the Virgin in Zaytoun; the Church of Marie Guirgis; and the Cathedral of St. Mark, the second largest church in Africa. The remains of St. Mark, the first to preach Christianity in Egypt, were removed to this cathedral. There is also The Virgin's Tree where the Virgin Mary is said to have rested with the child Jesus when they came to Egypt.

Egypt has many other Christian sites of interest. There are numerous shrines in the desert areas and in the oasis, particularly monasteries, since Egypt was one of the earliest sites of monks. Here also was the center of one of the biggest controversies in the Christian church: the crisis over whether Jesus was man or God. This debate led to a series of international meetings, including the Council of Nicea in 325 C.E.

Historic Islamic Monuments

The Islamic sites include thousands of mosques, so only the most famous will be mentioned here. The first is the Mosque of Amr Ibn Al-Aas, who was the Arab leader who came to help the Egyptians throw off the Roman law. There is also the Mosque of Ahmed Ibn Touloun, the Al-Azhar Mosque, the Mosque and Madrassa of Sultan Hassan, The Blue Mosque, the Mosque of al-Mu'ayyad, and the Alabaster Mosque of Muhammad Ali. There are other buildings that might hold interest for the reader, such as the Fortress of Salah ad Din al-Ayyubi—called Saladin in the West and known as The Citadel—and the House of Al-Seheimi. It is also possible to study the mosques of Egypt as a history of the country since the arrival of the Arabs in 639 C.E. because the mosques constitute the physical evidence of construction, reconstruction, and activity in various towns and cities during the conquest of Islam.

3

Religion and Worldview

RELIGION plays a major role in the life of the ordinary Egyptian. From the time one wakes in the morning until one goes to sleep at night, religion is a part of the average Egyptian's daily ritual. In fact, it is a way of life. Nothing in Egypt is untouched by religion. Thus, the political, economic, and cultural life of the people is impacted and influenced by the religious outlook. The official religion of Egypt is Islam. Soon after the establishment of the religion in Mecca, Arabs conquered Egypt in 639 C.E. and set up the first mosques in the country.[1] Since that time Islam has been the most dynamic religion in Egypt, becoming the dominant way of life barely one hundred years after the conquest.

Modern Egypt is essentially made up of the Islamic culture with limited or no regard to the ancient religion of the pharaohs. Although there is some official recognition of the ancient history, it does not figure in the ethics or morality of contemporary Egyptians. As far as the government is concerned, the Egypt of the pharaohs is an iconic part of the history that can be referred to, used, and exploited for tourists, but it is not a real part of the lives of the masses. In fact, the Egyptian people see the ancient monuments as a distraction from the piety that should be given to Allah.

The ordinary people of Egypt see their nation as a religious country, although there is a growing sentiment for the country to be secular, becoming in one sense, more like a Western republic. Islam is the major religion in Egypt, but freedom of religion is technically protected by the government. Since 91 percent of the people are Muslims, only 7 percent are Christians, and fewer than 2 percent are categorized as "Other," it is hardly any doubt

Mosque of Mohammad Ali

that the domination of the Islamic faith is all-encompassing. The Christians largely belong to the Coptic Orthodox Church, although there are a few Christians from other denominations. The word "Copt" comes from the Greek *Aeguptos* and applies to Christians of the Egyptian Church, whereas the Egyptian Catholic Church holds association with the Roman Catholic Church. One might encounter the names Egyptian Church, Egyptian Coptic Church, or Egyptian Orthodox Church, but they all refer essentially to the same people.

HISTORY

The final defeat of the Roman army under the command of Armenian General Manuel by Arab General El As marked the end of Roman rule and the beginning of the end for the Christian religion in Egypt. Although Coptic Christians had assisted El As in his campaign against the Romans, who had also been violently opposed to the Christian religion, the Copts did not know what awaited Christianity at the conclusion of the Arab conquest. While the Copts themselves were spared utter destruction because of their affiliation with the Arab conquerors, Christianity itself as a religion would only exist a few more years before Islam became the state religion. It should be pointed out that El As complained to the caliph that the Copts had been mistreated by some of the commanders although they had been allies in the defeat of the Romans. He ordered full compensation to be paid to the Copts for their losses (Butler 1902, 488). The suppression of Manuel and the recapture of Alexandria by the Arabs were perhaps the definitive moments of the establishment of Islam in the Nile Valley.

When El As had conquered Alexandria for the last time, he was ordered by the caliph to leave the country after only one month. The governance of the capital city of Egypt was turned over to Abdallah ibn Said. When the Romans, nine years after the conquest, tried to mount a fleet to retake Egypt, it was already too late: the Arabs had begun to master the sea-lanes as well. The Arab fleet met the Romans in the Mediterranean Sea and with the assistance of a mighty storm decimated the Roman army. This broke Roman power to challenge the new rulers of Egypt. With the exception of a few raids on the coastal towns by Byzantine pirates, the country of Egypt, at least around the Delta, was under the full sway of the Muslims.

The religious and social transformations that took place as a result of the conquest were remarkable. There was an almost swift decay of the Greco–Roman civilization in Egypt accompanied by a slow but steady growth of the religion of Islam. In one sense the religion of Islam must be seen as overlaying the Greco-Roman culture, which had tried to overlay the ancient African civilization that gave birth to the Pharaonic religion and society. Islam banished the traditional culture of the Greeks in Egypt—Coptic Christianity—to the convents and monasteries of the deserts.

It is possible to see how Islam and the Arabic culture spread over the country in the late 7th century by examining how Arabic first appeared in coins. From its use in coinage, the Arabic language was then used in public offices and public documents, quickly overtaking Coptic and totally driving out the Greek in ordinary common speech. Except for the few Greek words that took on an Arabic form or remain until this day embedded in the Coptic language Greek is essentially dead as a language in Egypt.

ISLAM

Islam came with the conquerors of Egypt and remains the religion of the vast majority of the Egyptian people today. It is a religion that is based on the principles laid down by its first and only prophet, Muhammad.

The Prophet Muhammad

Muhammad was born in Mecca around 570 C.E. At this time Mecca was gaining in popularity as a city with experienced caravan leaders. Meccans got permission from powerful kingdoms such as Abyssinia, Byzantium, and Persia for the caravans to traverse their territories and to transact business with those countries as well. Meccans made money when they provided escorts to foreigners passing through Arabia. While not interested much in the art of writing, Meccans cultivated arts such as poetry, oratory, and spoken discourses.

The social relationships between women and men were not tyrannical. Women were generally well treated and had the privilege of owning property. Furthermore, they gave consent to marriage contracts, and could add the condition of reserving their right to divorce their husbands. They could remarry when widowed or divorced.

It was in this context that Muhammad was born about three weeks after the death of his father, Abdallah (his grandfather raised him). As was the custom of the day, Muhammad was entrusted to a Bedouin, foster mother, and lived with her for several years in the desert. When the child was brought back home, his mother, Aminah, took him to his maternal uncles at Medina to visit his father's tomb. On the return trip, his mother died suddenly, and when he reached Mecca he found that his beloved grandfather had died as well. With such suffering and deprivation, Muhammad was placed in the care of his uncle Abu Talib. Although his uncle was generous, he did not have enough resources to support his own family. This condition led the young Muhammad out of the house to earn his livelihood as a shepherd boy. Then when he was ten, he accompanied his uncle on a caravan to Syria.

When Muhammad was about twenty-five, he established a reputation for honesty, integrity, and being of good character. It is no wonder that a rich woman took him in her employ and consigned to him her goods to be taken for sale to Syria. Soon Muhammad, the caravan agent, married Khadijah; she was forty and he was twenty-eight. Muhammad traveled to fairs in Yemen and Oman where he met traders from Abyssinia, Persia, India, and China.

The story is told among Muslims that one day a Yemenite improvised a satirical poem against some Meccans who had refused to pay him the price of what he had sold, and others who had not supported his claim or had failed to come to his help when he was beaten. Soon thereafter, Zuhair, one of Muhammad's uncles, felt great remorse when he heard this poem. He organized an order of chivalry (called *Hilf al-fudul*) with the objective of aiding the oppressed in Mecca, irrespective of whether they were dwellers of the city or aliens. Muhammad was an active member of the organization.

When Muhammad was about thirty-five there was a fire that destroyed the draperies of the walls of the Kaaba, a huge building in Mecca that is reported to have been established by Abraham. It was a building dedicated to the One God. The people started to reconstruct the Kaaba, and each person who had earned honest money was asked to contribute to the rebuilding process. (Muhammad's shoulders were injured while carrying heavy stones to the site.) A black stone was set in the wall to create a marker for the beginning place for circumambulation. There was competition among the citizens for the right to transport the stone to its proper place. The citizens almost came to blows and then it was suggested that they accept the arbitration of the person who arrived first at the site. It so happened that Muhammad—who was popularly known by the title *al-Amin* (the honest)—just then turned up for work as usual, and he became the arbitrator. He placed a large piece of cloth on the ground, put the stone on it, and asked the chiefs of all the clans in the city to lift the stone together so that it could be set in its proper place. According to the records from this moment, Muhammad became absorbed in spiritual meditations. In the tradition of his grandfather, he would retire during the whole month of Ramadan to a cave in Jabal-an-Nur ("Mountain of Light").

One night near the end of the month of Ramadan, after his fifth consecutive year making his retreats, an angel announced to Muhammad that God had chosen him as His messenger. The angel taught him the mode of ablutions: the way of worshipping God and the conduct of prayer. Shaken by the experience, the forty-year-old Muhammad returned home and related to his wife what had happened, expressing his fears that it might have been something diabolic or the action of evil spirits. Khadijah comforted him, saying that he had always been a man of kindness and generosity—helping the poor, the orphans, the widows, and the needy—and assured him that God would protect him against any evil thoughts or beings.

It would be another three years before the prophet would receive more revelations. He was told that God had not forsaken him and that he should take care of the orphans and the poor and to proclaim the bounty of God. Muhammad saw this as an order to preach. Another revelation directed him to warn people against evil practices, to exhort them to worship none but the One God, and to abandon everything that would displease God (Q. 74: 2–7). Yet another revelation commanded him to warn his own near relatives (Q. 26:214) and "Proclaim openly that which thou art commanded, and withdraw from the idolaters." While the first revelation came in his sleep, the subsequent ones came while he was fully awake.

Muhammad started his mission secretly, telling only his closest friends and relatives. He insisted on the belief in One Transcendent God, in Resurrection and the Last Judgment. He taught that all men must be generous and show beneficence. He took the necessary steps to preserve, through writing, the revelations he was receiving, and ordered his adherents to learn them by heart. The Qur'an was not received all at once, but in parts and fragments as the spirit revealed it to Muhammad.

But as the members grew in number, so did the intensity of the opposition. In fact, the opposition degenerated over the course of time into physical torture of the prophet and of those who had embraced his religion: they were stretched on burning sands, cauterized with red-hot iron, and imprisoned with chains around their ankles. Some of them died of the effects of torture, but none would renounce his religion. In despair, the Prophet Muhammad advised his companions to quit their native town and take refuge abroad, in Abyssinia, "where governs a just ruler, in whose realm nobody is oppressed." Dozens of Muslims profited by his advice as they fled to Abyssinia. However, everyone did not leave; those who remained in Mecca were persecuted even more. Tired of the persecution meted out by their neighbors, those who believed became devoted to the new religion and they practiced it with ardent passion. The Prophet Muhammad called the religion "Islam," meaning submission to the will of God.

The Qur'an and Islamic Law

The Qur'an is the holy scriptures of the Muslim faith. It contains the revelations made to Muhammad through the mediation of the archangel Gabriel. These teachings were communicated to Abu Bakr, who is reported to have written down the words of the prophet. The book contains a large amount of ethical teachings that comprise the foundation of the *shari'a*— discussed further in a later section. It is made up of legal injunctions, prohibitions, and precepts meant to assist humans in the proper way of living their lives. Notwithstanding the extensive instructions in the Qur'an, when they are not enough to provide explanations for various situations, a group of teachings called *Sunna* (habits) is called upon for further explanation. These traditions of authority contain the words and deeds of the prophet during his lifetime. Specific stories of activities of the prophet and his followers are called *Hadith* and form a strong body of expressions that are claimed to have come from the prophet.

Like most Islamic societies, Egyptian life is often deeply influenced by the four schools of Islamic law that take their names from the four founding teachers of the religion: *Hanafi* after Abu Hanafi, *Maliki* after Malik ibn Anas, *Shafi'i* after Al-Shafi'i, and *Hanbali* after Ahmad ibn Hanbali. Muslims accept these four schools of law as orthodox.

Islam had to overcome both the remnants of the ancient Egyptian religions and Christianity that had been established in Alexandria among the Copts almost seven hundred years earlier in order to assert its will over the Egyptian population. Thus, although Christianity remains in the form of the Coptic Church, Islam has imprinted every aspect of the society. A few Christian denominations are found in the country, but they are limited. While there is lip service to freedom of religion, there can be no official support for complete religious freedom, that is, opening the country up to missionaries and evangelists, such as one finds in other African countries where evangelical Christianity is generally left alone to flourish among the peasants. Egypt has tolerated the Coptic Church and some Roman Catholic congregations but it has not always been hospitable to other Christian denominations.

Older than Islam was the Jewish religion in Egypt. Jews had been in Egypt for many years before the arrival of the Christians and have continued in Egypt until the present. Several quite ancient synagogues still exist in Cairo despite the fact that they are often targets of bitterness. Egyptians generally accept the presence of Jews; however, the population often expresses anger at Israeli policies against the Palestinians. This causes the Egyptian Jewish population to be apprehensive and to remain low key in their activities.

The Five Pillars of Faith

The Muslim religion is based on the five pillars of faith: *shahada*, prayer, fasting, pilgrimage, and *zakat*. The pillars are clearly identified in the following practices:

1. The believer must confess that there is no God but God, and Muhammad is his prophet.
2. The believer must pray five times a day.
3. The believer must fast during the month of Ramadan.
4. The believer must make a pilgrimage, *hajj*, to Mecca during his lifetime.
5. The believer must give charity, *zakat*, to the poor.

The first pillar—*shahada*—emphasizes an all-encompassing monotheism and the belief that Muhammad is the prophet of Allah. The second pillar is prayer, and the Muslim believes that prayer can be offered anywhere a person can prostrate himself before Allah. There should be five prayers: at sunrise, at noon, afternoon, sunset, and at night. The most important prayer is the Friday noon prayer referred to as *salat el-Gomaa*. Fasting—the third pillar— is especially important for the ninth month of the Muslim year, called Ramadan. The idea behind fasting, according to the teaching, is restraint. Thus, a person is to observe complete abstinence from food and drink or smoking from the first sign of daybreak until sunset. A large meal may be taken after sunset (*Iftar*), and a lighter one is taken before going to bed, but not after dawn. Those who are ill or are traveling may be exempt from fasting, though they could still compensate by taking up fasting the exact number of days later in the year. Ramadan is observed as a holy month because the twenty-seventh of the month is the commemoration of the revelation of the first *surah* (chapter) of the Qur'an to the Prophet Muhammad. The fourth pillar is pilgrimage (*hajj*). Each believer is supposed to make a pilgrimage to the holy house of Mecca during the twelfth month of the Muslim year. The believer does not have to make the *hajj* if he is unable to do so financially or physically. During the *hajj* the believer puts on the Ihram garments: a white seamless cloth thrown across the body with the right arm and shoulder exposed. The pilgrim is prohibited from immoral acts or sexual intercourse during this time. The fifth pillar is *zakat* (charity, or the giving of alms), which is an outward sign of piety and a means of salvation. *Zakat* is seen as a loan to Allah that will be repaid a hundredfold. The believer is required to give a portion of his wealth to assist the poor as an obligation of Islam.

EGYPTIAN ISLAM

Those who practice Islam are usually referred to as Muslims. Egyptian Islam prohibits gambling, drinking alcohol, and eating pork. No images of the Prophet are permitted. Like most religions, Islam seeks to provide moral guidance to all believers. The prohibitions on certain behaviors are meant to ensure a healthy and productive society. There are no priestly classes, as such, in Islam. Instead, the religion has mosque leaders (*imams*) who are selected for their adherence to the faith, exemplary conduct, and pious behavior, as well as their knowledge and practice of the Five Pillars of Faith. Islamic scholars (*ulama*) are responsible for deep study of the Qur'an and can issue edicts on various aspects of the doctrine of Islam. They are particularly useful in giving authoritative verdicts (*fatwas*) regarding disputes of doctrine and interpretation.

In Egypt there are two principal sects of Islam: Sunni and Shiite. The dispute between the sects over the line of succession to the Prophet Muham-mad is the central reason for the difference. The Shiites believe that Ali, the fourth of the prophet's successors, carries the legitimate line of the succession rather than the prophet's three companions: Abu Bakr, Omar, and Osman. While both principal Muslim groups believe in the Five Pillars of Faith, they are able to find sufficient reasons for disagreements over the interpretations of the religion to cause outbreaks of violence.

The Sufi Orders

Egyptians are very religious and they take Islam seriously. There are two expressions of religious practice in the country: the official Islam of Al-Azhar Mosque and the popular Islam of the masses of Egyptians. One is the religion of the leadership of the country, and the other is the religion of the humblest believers.

For generations, concurrent with the Islam of the mosque has been the *sufi* (mystic) Islam. The practitioners of *sufi* turn to a more direct interaction with God, believing that the mosque is too formalistic and tends to keep God away from the people. When men grouped themselves into *sufi* orders— or *tariqas* (paths)—they were establishing a way to express a more direct Islam. Egypt has dozens of these *sufi* groups, all under the High Sufi Council.

The *sufi* orders have attracted far more peasants than elites. Perhaps as a means of finding comfort, those who feel threatened by the society's rapid changes join the *sufi* orders. Loyalty to the *sufi* order and spiritual bonding are expressed in meetings that are called *dhikrs*. At these meetings rituals are performed in which the name of Allah is repeated hundreds of times to rhythmic drumming in a mystical manifestation of religious connection. Each member of the order seeks to achieve the ideal state whereby there is perfect union between the devotee and God. Some followers have been known to mumble the various formulas for long hours, cutting themselves on the arms and legs until they are quite bloody.

Like all religious orders, the *sufi* orders have holidays in which they celebrate special occasions in the religion. Among the most important celebrations is *mawlid* (the birthday) of a *sufi* saint. This is usually a big festival for the entire community. The largest of these festivals is that of Ahmad al-Badawi who died in Tanta in the year 1276. Every October his tomb becomes the center of a massive celebration and community fair. During this celebratory period people can visit the tomb and receive blessings from the saint. They could also enjoy the festive spirit at the celebration where booths, cafés, fireworks, bands, stalls, and processions are displayed in honor of the saint. Another celebration is the Feast of the Sacrifice. This occasion marks the killing of a sheep during the pilgrimage to Mecca. Perhaps a third celebration that the *sufi* orders recognize is the ending of the month of Ramadan. Many times the government takes advantage of these festivals to mingle politics with religion by illuminating photographs of national leaders under festive arches that show the name of Allah in lights.

SHARI'A

In many Islamic societies the only law that need be followed is *shari'a*. It is a law based on the Qur'an and the teachings and interpretations of Muhammad. According to the believers, the *shari'a* law covers all aspects of human life, although there are some provisions that might be augmented from customary law. So many issues have confronted modern societies that it has become increasingly difficult for Qur'anic law to answer all issues. Thus, in Egypt, as in other countries, lawyers have introduced secular law alongside the Islamic law.

Egypt, because of its many cultural infusions, also has a long tradition of secular law. This tradition goes back hundreds of years and was meant to regulate most aspects of public life, such as commercial and criminal issues. In fact, officially the legal system is based on English common law, Islamic law, and Napoleonic codes. Furthermore, judicial review by the Supreme Court and Council of State serve as a further layer of protection for the public.

However, legal issues and problems of marriage, divorce, and land inheritance are left to the *shari'a* court. By 1956 the *shari'a* courts of Egypt were fully integrated into the national system. The *ulama* allowed this move to occur without much opposition largely because they had seen how the court system functioned in Cairo where the *shari'a* was not particularly affected by secular law.

Secularization, however, has produced new calls for Arab nationalism as well as a revival in Islam. The political aspects of such revival, as in the Muslim Brotherhood, increased throughout the 1990s. Various sheikhs have used the religious platform to increase the membership of their organizations. They have offered a vision of society that is away from secularization and toward more reliance on the Islamic traditions.

Immediately after the September 11, 2001 World Trade Center and Pentagon terror attacks, Islamic militants and fundamentalists repeated the call for assaults on all forms of Americanism. While the overwhelming majority of Egyptians, according to the press, followed the national leaders in expressing condolences to the Americans for the tragedies, some imams, sympathizing with Osama bin Laden and his Egyptian colleagues in Afghanistan, urged Muslims to join a *jihad*, holy war, against America.

THE COPTS

The Copts are a large minority who are neither Muslim nor Arab. To the degree that they are non-Arabs they are like the Egyptian Nubians who represent the other member of the original family of Egypt. However, unlike the Nubians, the Copts have maintained their churches. The Copts are descendants of the first Egyptian Christians. Although the historical records show that many of them were of Greek descent from Alexandria, they gradually became integrated into the society. Whether ruled by Arab or Ottoman Muslims, the Copts kept their religion, faith, and educational curriculum. However, they abandoned their language and adopted Arabic. It is only the church leaders that still speak the Coptic language.

There is a respectable tolerance of each other between the Copts and the Muslims. In Upper Egypt, Muslim women observe the Spring Christian festival, at which ancient rites are performed just before Easter Sunday. Special foods are prepared and eaten. This is considered an Egyptian festival, and so Muslims participate in it much like non-Muslims participate in the many Muslim festivals held in the country.

Copts normally claim to be one-sixth of the population and as such have often sought to have more of a say in government. They have staked their case on their long affiliation as Egyptians and their service to the nation during historical events. However, many Egyptian leaders have been cautious about using too many Copts in the government. This has often strained relationships between Arabs and Copts. Under President Gamal Abdel Nasser there was little sympathy for the Copts. He was an Arab nationalist and failed to appoint Copts to any major high post during his administration. It seems that Nasser, while recognizing the Copts as national citizens, did not see them as cooperating with the ordinary, peasant farmers of Egypt. They were mainly urbanized cosmopolitans who identified with the industrial and business elite of the society.

The Copts have survived through horrendous harassment, discrimination, and persecution. They retained their religion and became engineers, lawyers, doctors, and teachers who have contributed to the Egyptian society. They have clung to their family traditions while respecting those of Islam. This attachment to Christianity is a reminder to the Muslims that all Egyptians did not accept the doctrine of Muhammad. In some ways, it is a thorn in the side of the Islamic culture.

There has always been a political interpretation to the population of Copts. The government seeks to minimize the numbers, while the Copts have always tried to increase the numbers. It is believed that there are at least 12 million Copts in Egypt. It is difficult to say exactly how many there are because peasant families like to keep the number of children they have secret. Some Copts think that the government does not consider their rural population—counting only the urbanized Coptic people. One thing is certain. Copts believe that they are underrepresented in the national government. During the time of Nasser, Islam was declared to be the religion of the state. Under the various reign of foreigners, Islam had coexisted with other religions, and although it was dominant for many years, it had not been declared the state religion. Nasser's willful attempt to impose the Muslim faith as the identity of the national state created problems for many other religious groups. Nevertheless, Copts demonstrated their loyalty to Nasser but still believed that he regarded them with indifference. This was to change somewhat under Anwar Sadat and Hosni Mubarak, who each appointed a few more Copts in the national government. None of these changes in government positions has actually changed the status of the Copts in the society. They are still looked upon as a minority, remain discriminated against because they are not Islamic, and have often been criticized by the national leaders.

Fundamentalist Islamic groups have attacked the Copts openly. Bombs have been planted outside of Coptic churches, and Coptic leaders have been threatened. In fact, during Sadat's administration the Coptic community protested against harassment only to be rebuked by Sadat who told them to stop playing politics. Sadat later had the head of the Coptic Church arrested.[2]

THE ISLAMIC DEFINITION OF THE SOCIETY

The practice of Islam in Egypt is the dominant religious belief system. Although the vast majority of the people are Muslim they share their society's spiritual space with several smaller faiths. However, it is Islam, above all, that defines the unique qualities of the Egyptian society. Because of its ubiquitous nature, the religion of Islam dictates social customs and commercial behaviors. Everyone who lives in the country is aware of the prohibitions of the religion and the values of maintaining the special qualities of the faith.

Yet this does not prevent Egypt from having some very significant modern activities. Cairo and Alexandria remain two of the most fashion-conscious cities in Africa. Ingy Yassin, who is Egyptian–Lebanese, is a young contemporary designer with a distinctive elegance and taste, but who keeps the Islamic motifs and icons in all of her fashions. One can discover in the works of modern artists such as Dr. Farouk Shehata, Dr. Sneed Heddaya, Dr. Adel El-Masri, and Dr. Attia Hussein—Alexandrians all—a respect for traditions but a strong overture to the contemporary world. Thus, faith in Egypt, while often breeding fundamentalists, does not have to mean abandonment of the modern world. Those who practice the most fundamental forms of Islam end up hating not only the "infidels" but those of their own religion who do not share their views. In Egypt this has led to intrareligious fights between devotees of the religion. Dogmatism and fundamentalism tend to lead to the disregard for the opinions of others.

MAJOR HOLIDAYS

There are a number of holidays celebrated in Egypt. The country recognizes three calendars: the Hijri (Islamic), the Gregorian (European) calendar, and the Coptic calendar. The Hijri calendar is lunar with twelve months of twenty-nine or thirty days and is ten or eleven days shorter than the Gregorian calendar. The Coptic calendar is a solar calendar with thirty days in a month and five days in the thirteenth month.

Most of the holidays—holy days—are related to religious observances. Christmas is observed on January 6 and 7. It begins on the night of the sixth when the Coptic Christians leave their homes and go to the churches at about 10 o'clock for the holy mass, and around midnight they have a large feast, usually involving the eating of a turkey. The next morning, they exchange gifts, and the young children are sent out to visit their grandparents and have lunch at the homes of their grandparents or other relatives.

Egyptians also observe the holiday of *Sham el-Nessim*, which is celebrated immediately after Easter. It is, therefore, always on Monday. The people of Egypt have celebrated this holiday (Spring Day) for more than 4,500 years. It is called *Sham el-Nessim* because the harvest season in ancient Egypt was called *Shamo*. In Arabic the word *Sham*—a shortened form of *Shamo*—means "to smell" and the words *el-Nessim* mean "the air," so literally the expression is "to smell the air." The early Egyptians offered salted fish, lettuce, eggs, and onion to the deities during this festival. Now, the same kinds of food are eaten but there is no offering made to Ra, Amen, Atum, or Ptah. On that day, however, the modern Egyptians say that lettuce represents hopefulness at the beginning of the spring. Eggs are used to represent the renewal of life in the season of the spring. People dye the eggs in various colors in a tradition that goes back to the ancient Egyptians who were probably the first to introduce this practice. Salted fish represents fertility and welfare.

Another holiday celebrated in Egypt is called *Eid el-Fetr*, a festival that comes after Ramadan. People eat special cookies. A special Muslim version of this holiday is called the *Eid el-Adha*, that is, festival of sacrifice. It is a four-day holiday. On the first day at dawn all the men go to the mosque to pray. Every family is supposed to slaughter a sheep, which they will have bought the day before, and take some of the meat to donate to the poor. The celebrants have breakfast that includes *fata* (a mixture of meat, bread, rice, and vinegar). Then the youth or younger people visit the older people in the community and eat food with them. The remaining three days of the festival is one big feast after another at the home of relatives.

On October 6, the nation celebrates Armed Forces Day. This is the celebration of the brilliant Egyptian tactical move of crossing into the Sinai in 1973. Such was the psychological lift that this military action gave to the nation that the Egyptian people were eager to make it an important holiday, an example of the nation in its finest military moment.

There is also the Islamic holiday *Mulid el-Nabawy* that points to the holy day of the Prophet Muhammad's birth. It is celebrated by making special candies and selling them in the streets and at stores throughout the country. The candies are pink and are usually in the shape of a horse or a doll. People normally wear their best clothes on this holiday. Families get together to celebrate, and decorations are found on the streets and buildings. In some senses, *Mulid el-Nabawy* is equivalent to Christmas.

NOTES

1. The conquest of Egypt under General El As began in 639 C.E. but went on for nearly five years. In fact, El As found it most difficult to pacify the Upper Egyptians around Aswan. "An expedition which [El As] sent against the Nubians [did] not merely [fail] to vanquish them, but was forced to retreat, having suffered much loss from the exceptional skill of the Nubian archers, whom the Arabs henceforth distinguished as the 'eye wounders' " (Butler 1992, 432). By 644 when El As delivered a sermon at the mosque named after him, all of Egypt had come under Arab domination and he could thank Allah for blessing his victories.

2. It is important to see the work of Hopwood (1982, 165) in this regard. He clearly shows that the Copts were in serious trouble with the government of Sadat. There is some belief that the Copts thought themselves superior to the rest of the population by virtue of their relationship to the ancient language of Egypt.

4

Architecture and Art

ARCHITECTURE

ONE WOULD THINK that a country as old as Egypt would have had many architectural influences. However, the architecture of modern Egypt is primarily influenced by Islamic culture.[1] Thus, to speak of how Egyptians build their homes and their great public buildings is to identify the way they make their identity concrete in the modern era. Architecture is a unique human activity that provides for landmarks of historical achievement in a people's culture. The environment is changed, altered in ways that establish a certain response to the natural spaces around us when architecture is practiced. Hence, Egyptian architecture, taking its main lead from the Islamic religion, has certain identifying characteristics.

First, it is an architecture that concerns itself more with interior spaces than with exterior spaces. Enclosed space that is bounded by walls, vaults, and arcades is the most important element of Egyptian architecture based on the Islamic model. The only exterior areas that are decorated are the dome and the entrance portal; the rest of the decoration is reserved for the interior. Second, unlike ancient Egyptian architecture, modern Islamic architecture does not emphasize the actual mechanics of a structure but rather concentrates on architectural decoration that de-emphasizes the reality of weight or the necessity for structural support. The third element that sets Islamic architecture apart is the variety of designs used to produce a sense of unlimited space and lightness. On walls and pillars, an architect uses mosaics of tiles, painted decorations of polychrome, and thousands of variations based on calligraphy, geometric shapes, and floral patterns to create architectural styles that are unknown in any other part of the world. Islamic architecture is specific to the religious culture out of which it is derived. It could be noted without exaggeration that the endless repetitive designs, floral patterns, and geometric forms on the walls of buildings create the idea of infinity that complements the vast array of arches, colonnades, rooms, and passages in the interiors of the great public buildings of Egypt.

The city of Cairo is one of the nine or ten cities in the world that might be called a "museum of a civilization." Like Florence, Philadelphia, Kumasi, New York, Kyoto, London, Boston, Beijing, Paris, or Rome, Cairo is itself the seat of a national and cultural reservoir of beauty and art. The history of Islam is told in the narrative of Cairo as an Arabic city. It has more than eight hundred buildings dating from the eleventh century, which was the period of Islam's fastest growth. It is still called the "City of 1000 Minarets" because of the numerous mosques built in every section of the city. Cairo is a jewel of Islamic architecture.

There are hundreds of historical buildings in Cairo. One such building is the Museum of Islamic Art that contains one of the largest collections of ceramics in the world. It is also a center for ancient manuscripts and a collection of beautiful woodwork. However, of all the historical buildings in Cairo, the mosques seem to dominate in terms of architectural importance, as if one builder was trying to outdo the next. The Mosque of Ibn Tulun is one of the largest in the world. Some critics even think that it is the best mosque in Cairo. It was built between 876 and 879 C.E. in a plain, straightforward, powerful style. It attracts visitors from all over the world.

A person visiting Cairo can cross the Tahrir Bridge (flanked by two bronze lions at either end) onto Gezira Island and visit the Cairo Opera House, which was opened in 1988, as well as the city's most famous landmark (after the pyramids), the 614–foot-high Cairo Tower built in 1961. The tower features a popular restaurant from which one can view the city below. Looking out over the many minarets of the city, one is impressed by the many cultures that have contributed to Cairo's image as the "Mother of the World."

The Khan el-Khalili Bazaar, bordered by Al-Azhar and Muski Streets, is a massive shopping area consisting of hundreds of small shops along numerous winding alleyways. It is a thirteenth-century marketplace in the middle of a twenty-first century city. The huge market was established in 1292 and has been in service since that time with craftsmen still plying their traditional crafts in the narrow streets. At the Wikalet el-Ghouri—across from the Sharia Muski market area (similar to the Khan el-Khalili) and next to the Al-Azhar Mosque—there is a school that teaches crafts. Students come to the school to learn the basic art of making baskets, painting hieroglyphics on pottery and jewelry, and jewelry making.[2]

Khan el-Khalili is the bargain center for leather, glass, gold, silver, and spices. In Cairo, the other main downtown areas for shopping are Talaat Harb, Qarr el-Nil and 23rd of July Streets. Egyptian society is a market culture and all major towns have markets; some, such as the Aswan Market with its spices, are specialized. Cairo, on the other hand, as the supreme capital has markets that contain products and produce from all over the country.

All architecture in Egypt is not on a grand public scale. There is the ordinary architecture of the everyday house. Like the large public buildings, the house is also based on the creation of interior space. Rectangular housing units are always organized according to this principle of focus on interior spaces. This is most often shown when one looks at the role of the courtyard in Egyptian homes. The outside of the house offers only a small door. It is usually windowless on the front, giving the impression of a *mastaba* (a rectangularly shaped box).

It is even useful to think of the house as a courtyard or courtyards connected to apartments. In this way one gains an appreciation for the complexity of the design as a house. Whereas the Western house is usually a collection of rooms attached to each other with an occasional hallway, the Egyptian house might be thought of as a massively expanded corridor with rooms coming into it.

The houses in the rural areas, and in some sections of the urban communities, might be clustered together so that large families can be accommodated. These courtyard houses are usually within a walled complex and are meant to contain an extended family. They are expandable should other members need housing. One enters the complex through a single door that leads to a corridor from which an apartment might be reached. Egyptian families are accustomed to adding on to their courtyard clusters until all of the land around the main cluster is used up. When that is accomplished, the building goes upward to accommodate still more family members.

There is one other feature of the traditional Egyptian house that must be mentioned. Since there is male privilege in Egypt and the male head of the household often has male guests, it is necessary that the house be constructed in such a way that a male visitor does not violate the harem or come into contact with the wives of the host. Thus, the house is "divided in two" by a wall separating the male section from the female section, and the male guest room is usually located near the entrance lobby. (The Arab nomads used to hang a screen or a rug down the middle of the tent to separate the males from the females.) While many of these types of houses still exist, it seems as if Western influences are coming into play in many constructions. Some styles of architecture are creating novel ways of separating men and women in terms of sleeping and working spaces, while keeping the Western influences of convenience and efficiency.

Architecturally, the Egyptian house is an advanced structure. The open-air interior allows air to circulate to all of the apartments that are connected to the courtyard. It is a system that regulates the flow of air and assists in climate control in the hot, dry climate. It also serves as an air well where the cool night air can penetrate the various corridors and apartments heated by the sun. Much like the public buildings, the ordinary house has a thick-walled front façade that is designed to withstand the sun and wind. Most roofs are flat and they have high parapets. One can pick out an Egyptian house usually by the characteristic designs on the roof line.

Sometimes this architecture of the courtyard is referred to as the "architecture of the veil." Because it is enclosed by a plain façade and is the inner-most area of the house, the courtyard is "kept as a secret." One never knows what awaits when entering a courtyard. There one could find children playing, elders in conversation, or family celebrations. What is being expressed by this type of housing design is the need to keep the outside world out while protecting the family deep inside the walls. The private house uses the concealed-courtyard style of architecture as a defining characteristic. The feature also appears in nonresidential structures. In fact, most architecture in Egypt, like that in many Islamic communities, is not function specific. You might use the same structure for several functions or you might create a form that can serve a variety of purposes because there is an absence of specific architectural forms for specific functions. One good example is the four-*iwan* design. An *iwan* is an arched opening or porch reached from a central court-yard. Many buildings use the four-*iwan* model. Yet one can easily see that this design can be adapted to homes, mosques, palaces, and modern buildings such as banks and museums. This allows the user of the structure to adapt it to their functions despite the form.

In many ways the modern Egyptian architecture is different from the old architecture of Pharaonic Egypt. One sees the difference expressed in one of the principal features of Islamic buildings in which there is no inherent concern for directional quality. Thus, whereas the ancient temples were developed along axial lines with directional quality being at the center of the structure, Islamic buildings may have a different quality that ignores the notion of directionality. One could enter a building without being pointed directly to the main area of function. Such is the case when you enter a building from the side where there is an altar that could have more easily, in the ancient sense, been reached by heading straight-on toward it from the directional front.

Looking at the grand architecture in Cairo and Alexandria, one gets the impression that there is a convivial meeting of materials, ideas, and techniques when the builders create a structure along the Islamic path. It is not possible to ascertain a lot of information about some of the earlier architects in Egyptian history, but it is known that they had to study geometry, mathematics, and drawing to develop the skills they mastered in the construction of the large public buildings.

Most of the great mosques were erected during the lifetimes of the architects—unlike many of the greatest buildings in the West where the architect who conceived a project may not be the one who completed it. Among the Islamic builders this was rare. They built quickly and without many of the financial constraints of the Western nations. If an emperor or king wanted a building built, he would not have to consult with anyone. The rulers were often quite dictatorial and could demand that a building be erected within a certain period of months.

The organization of the trades to build was a key element in being able to complete a project on time. Sawyers were used to prepare the rough timber to the correct dimensions; carpenters were called in to detail most of the woodwork in the buildings; turners were used to make wooden screens for windows; carvers were those who decorated and worked with precious stones, woods, ivory, and mother-of-pearl.

Similar to the woodworkers, the quarrymen were also divided into specialties. Some prepared the rough stones for inner walls and foundations; skilled carvers helped to finish some of the stone blocks; masons were used for the rough stonework on the inner walls; and other masons were used for the rough inner and outer cores between the outer and inner faces of the walls. Other important tradespeople included bricklayers, clay-wallers, metal-workers, and plasterers.

The minaret—a tall, slender tower on a mosque—is one of the most visible expressions of Islamic art. It is used by the *muezzin* (a Muslim crier) to summon the people to pray. Climbing to the top of the minaret, the *muezzin* calls the faithful to the hour of prayer. Minarets were first built as low, square towers used for pagan and Islamic rituals, such as in the case of the Syrian minarets that existed before the Islamic era. Islamic architects built them taller to afford the *muezzin* a greater opportunity to call people to pray. The common form of minaret has a square base, topped by several stories, and then a balcony constructed out of balsam wood. This "square plan" minaret has been developed further: the tower is crowned by a dome or a conical roof.

FINE ARTS

Most scholars date the origins of the modern Egyptian fine arts to the year 1904. In that year the city of Alexandria accepted 210 paintings and the sum of 500 gold pounds from a German art dealer, Edward Friedham, with the stipulation that the city would start a museum. Soon thereafter the municipality created the Museum of Fine Arts of Alexandria, rented an apartment on Fouad Street, and opened for business. Baron Charles de Menasha donated a villa to house the museum in 1926. When the Revolutionary Government came to power, it placed its stamp of approval on the Museum of Fine Arts in 1954. A year later the city of Alexandria held the first Biennial for Mediterranean Countries in order to link art and culture in the various countries. The aim of this gathering was to emphasize what each country had in common with its Mediterranean neighbor because of the common geographical and historical experiences. Soon thereafter the Revolutionary Government opened a Faculty of Fine Arts under the direction of the black Egyptian sculptor Ahmed Othman, one of the most distinguished of Egyptian artists.[3]

In 1908, Prince Youssef Kamal created the first School of Fine Arts in Egypt on Darb el Gamamiz Street in Cairo. One of the first students was the great sculptor Mahmoud Mukhtar. All of the teachers at the School of Fine Arts were foreigners. No Egyptians were permitted to teach since the idea was to prepare Egyptians for the Western world.

The school soon came under the control of the national university and was joined to the Arts Education Department in the Ministry of Education as well. The school was moved to another location in 1926. By this time the tensions running in the school were quite high because the Egyptians believed that the school should be "Egyptianized" in staff and content. Efforts were made to hire more Egyptian faculty members, and the school became a high school until 1950. Then it was called the Royal Faculty of Fine Arts until 1961 when it became a part of the national Ministry of Higher Education. By 1975 it had regained its status as an arts faculty and joined the Helwan University.

Early on in Egypt there was a distinction made in the arts between the applied arts and the fine arts. In fact, in 1909 the School of Fine Arts opened a section called "Applied Arts" to deal with decorative arts and crafts. By 1918, it had become independent and went by the name The School of Egyptian Decorative Arts. In 1941, the name was changed to Higher School of Applied Arts. By 1950 the school had undergone yet another change in names, and it was now called the Royal Higher Faculty for Applied Arts.

Women students were permitted for the first time in the 1956–1957 school year.

Egypt was not unlike other countries under the control of dominating nations. So when the First World War ended, a group of teachers was sent to London in 1920 to study how to draw. In this first group was Habib Gorgi, a mathematics teacher turned artist, who specialized in arts education. He played a major role in getting fellow students through the course in England. About this time a Department of Fine Arts—which became the Ministry of Culture after the Revolutionary Government instituted it in 1958—was created in the Ministry of Education in Cairo. Habib Gorgi's influence was powerful during the early years of arts development in Egypt because he was a leader in arts education, teaching many of the greatest artists in Egyptian history. The Institute of Art Education was established in Cairo in 1937. Its name was changed to the Faculty of Art Education and added to the Helwan University.

In 1976, an artists' guild was established by the government when it enacted Law No. 83. The same year another decree ordered that a Faculty of Fine Arts be created at Minya in Upper Egypt.

The fine arts in Egypt were encouraged by an unlikely source. When Ragheb Ayyad went to Rome in 1924 on a mission, he was impressed by the quality of students that had come from other countries to study art. Ayyad was instrumental in getting the government to set up the Egyptian Academy of Arts in Rome. In 1929, that academy was formally established, and the artist Shehab Almaz was appointed director.

Egyptian governments have tried to do what they could to encourage art appreciation. In 1975, a law was passed that granted a state prize for creativity to encourage artists to work. However, by 1984 only four artists had benefitted from the award, which was to study at the Egyptian Academy of Arts in Rome. It was only when Farouk Hosni, an artist, became Minister of Culture in 1987 that a new law was enacted that implemented changes that brought about results.

Egypt's modern history is one of trying to gather in the rich legacies of the past and make them the work for the present and future. In this regard the country has been somewhat successful with a parade of outstanding artists. While Egypt is without peer in the area of ancient art and architecture, it has not enjoyed the same stature in contemporary art. The fine arts tradition, in the Western way, has been slow to emerge given the tremendous strength of Egypt's classical history. Yet the great artists have created works equal to that of any other artists anywhere in the world.

The General Department for Museums became a part of the Ministry of

Culture in 1966. It had been formed in 1959 during a period of consolidation. To give it more support, the government encouraged it to become a part of the Ministry of Culture. Abdul Qader Rizk, director of the art museums, began a tradition of holding a General National Plastic Arts Exhibition to allow new artists to demonstrate their versatility and creativity. Rizk wanted the exhibition to bring together the makers and the buyers of art. His idea was that individuals and corporations would bring joint interests in art to the exhibition and both parties would benefit.

When Rizk retired in 1972, Abdul Hamid Hamdi became director of the General Department of Fine Arts and National Museums. Under the directorship of Hamdi, the name of the department was changed to the General Authority for Arts and Literature, consisting of the Academy of Arts and two Departments for Literature and Special Creativity Grants. His aim was to give artists enough leisure time to devote energy to creating art.[4]

Changes occur somewhat constantly in the art world in Egypt. It is a country of dynamic art movements, many being initiated by new artists who are influenced by outside artistic movements, but most coming from sources inside the country and inspired by the government agencies themselves. Soon after the creation of the General Authority for Arts and Literature, the Supreme Council for Culture was instituted and became, in 1980, the generator of all arts programs. The Supreme Council for Culture created the National Centre for Plastic Arts to handle the activities of the previous General Authority for Arts and Literature. This was a major step for the country because it brought legitimacy to the many works and activities of the artists who had worked on their own.

Cairo Museums

Cairo is famous for the huge Egyptian Museum of Antiquities. No other museum in the world compares with it. In many ways it is the definition of the term "art," for most people who consider Egyptian art. This has been a major problem for modern art and artists. Overshadowed by the ancient world in such a massive way, the fine arts tradition has gone through many shifts, trends, and organizations in an effort to stabilize and popularize the artistic professions and traditions. Nevertheless, there is, and has been for a long time, a museum dedicated to the fine arts.

The most momentous, yet characteristic, act to advance the fine arts tradition in Egypt was the creation in 1930 of the Cairo Museum of Modern Art. It was located in the Mosseiri Palace on Fouad I Street, now called 26th July Street. Seven years later this museum was moved to the center of the city and located in the palace of Hoda Shaarawi near Bab el Louk. A few years later it was moved to the palace of Count Zogheib in Kasr el Nil Street. This palace was demolished in 1964 to make way for a hotel, which in 2001 still had not been built. The museum had to be moved again, and, thus, it was taken to a villa in Finny Square in Dokki where it remained until it was located in a new building in Gezireh between the Cairo Opera House and the Plastic Arts Guild. The challenge of a fine arts museum was undertaken in Cairo long after one had been set up in Alexandria. This was critical for the growth of fine arts in the country, but the instability in locations was an indication of how insecure the tradition was for a period of time. Finding a place where the arts could flourish proved to be something that Egyptians did not see as a priority in earlier times.

The Revolutionary Government came to power in 1952 with the idea of opening national art museums. The leaders were literally full of ideas. In some ways they represented the spirit of transformation that was sweeping the world and would cause the Western nations to pause and admire the energy and artistic abilities of the newly independent and freed nations. Egypt's Nasser was a visionary, not unlike Kwame Nkrumah of Ghana would be in 1957 when his country gained its independence. These were men who believed that their countries could do and be anything the people desired them to be. In Nasser's case, he wanted Egypt to be in the forefront of the world's nations and did not subscribe to the idea that Egypt had to remain a third-rate nation in any field. As in energy, so it was to be in art; Egypt was to reach for the top in everything it did. By 1959, the government had opened two museums: the Gawwad Hosni Museum in Port Fouad and the National Resistance Museum in Port Said. In 1960, two other museums were created: the National Mansoura Museum (Dar ibn Luqman) and the Denshway Museum in Monofiya Governorate. In 1962, it opened the museums of Mahmoud Khalil, Gezireh, and Mahmoud Mukhtar in Cairo. In May 1968, another museum was set up in the Pyramids Quarter and was called Mohamed Nagui Museum; and in 1972, the Mahmoud Said Museum was established in Alexandria.[5] Egypt had finally found its way to the creation of a group of museums reflective of the contemporary history of the nation.

The Museum of Mahmoud Mukhtar at the Huriyya Gardens was designed by the great architect Ramses Wissa Wassef to house the works of the pioneer in modern Egyptian sculpture that the museum was named for. The same year—1962—the Museum of Mohamed Mahmoud Khalil was opened and his large collection of European impressionists was displayed.

When President Anwar Sadat took office in 1970 the contents of the Museum of Mohamed Mahmoud Khalil were moved to the Amr Ibrahim Palace in Zamalek and the building was taken over by the presidency. By July 1975, the public was invited to a reopening of the museum in its new quarters. Farouk Hosni, as Minister of Culture, was able to get the contents of this museum moved back to its original quarters after the inauguration of President Hosni Mubarak. Mubarak opened the museum once again in 1995.

National Galleries

Although the country had established a number of museums, including the early Alexandria museum and the Cairo museum, until 1966 it only had two public galleries where people could come to view the works of new artists. Those two galleries, run by the Ministry of Culture, were the Fine Arts Gallery in the Chamber of Commerce in Bab al Louk and the Akhenaten Gallery. Both were rented spaces. The Ministry of Culture soon opened two additional galleries in the headquarters of the Socialist Union and one more in the Gezireh Fair Grounds that was called Nile Hall. By 1967, it was clear that there was a demand for galleries as the public expressed its will to purchase art and the artists wanted to sell their works. An annual bazaar for selling works of art was started, but it is believed that social or religious pressures brought the practice to an end within a few years.

Many artists decided to travel abroad to perfect their work. Mohamed Abdul Monem Murad went to France in 1967 to study painted fabrics. Upon his return, a project was started at the Rakayib Museum in Helwan. France agreed to give grants to Egyptian artists to study textile painting at the Aubusson Institute in France. When they returned, they created beautiful textiles under the supervision of Murad Ghalib. Although the process by which the works of artists is viewed by the public seems difficult at times, the work continues and the artists are making a tremendous headway in the plastic arts field.

KEY ARTISTS

Ahmed Othman and Mahmoud Mukhtar stand as two of the great columns of modern Egyptian sculpture. Othman is regarded more as an administrator of art, a guiding force in the world of sculpture, and a singularly impressive genius at discovering within Egyptian materials all of the emotions. Mukhtar is regarded as the national spirit combined with classical and Western styles as seen in his work *Nahdat Misr* (Egypt Awakening), *The Guard of the Fields*, and *The Bride of the Nile*. His works are found throughout Cairo.

One cannot speak of the foundations of Egyptian painting without mentioning the name of Ragheb Ayyad who lived from 1892 until 1982, spanning a great part of the modern period of Egyptian art. In fact, Ayyad was so inspired by the fact that Egypt had such a glorious pharaonic heritage that he tried to emulate the tradition by painting the ordinary activities of the people in the countryside: fishing, farming, and working in various industries. A contemporary of his, Yusef Kamel, who lived from 1891 until 1971, often painted scenes of the landscape of Egypt. He liked very much to paint the way the light was reflected in the colors of the flowers in the fields, the plants in the gardens, trees alongside the Nile, and the beautiful Egyptian sunlight beaming down on some lonely farmer or boatman. Both Ayyad and Kamel might be called impressionistic artists. They were not alone, however, in their emphasis on the ordinary experiences of Egyptians. Other artists, particularly Ahmed Sabri (1889–1955), Mohamed Hassan (1892–1961), Othman Murtada (1896–1925), and Mahmoud Hassan (1899–1955) made enormous contributions to the development of modern Egyptian art. Sabri painted people with great sensitivity to their faces, seeking to bring out their innermost experiences, and to establish the human presence as an enduring visual experience. Mohamed Hassan was the intellectual among painters. His style was exact, precise, and he loved to use the proper colors and lines to make holistic compositions. Murtada and Mahmoud Hassan were sculptors whose work dealt with numerous modern figures in Egyptian art and culture. Their works added to the value of the Egyptian Wax Museum.

A second generation of artists was trained by the School of Fine Arts and became leaders in the art establishment of Egypt after the 1940s: the sculptors Salah Abdul Kerim, Mahmoud Moussa, and Abdul Hamid Hamdi; the painters Hosni al Banani and Kamel Mustafa; and in graphics and ceramics, Kamal Amin and Hassan Sadek. Some of these artists were fortunate enough to be attached to an atelier in Luxor in 1942 where they were encouraged to move among the ancient monuments for inspiration. The atelier was later closed and the artists were left to their own devices. In some ways this deepened their gifts as artists because they were no longer overly influenced by the genius of the past. Many went on to create great works of art.

Women have not been absent from the cultural life of Egypt. In fact, Effat Nagui was one of the best painters of her generation. Her brother Mohamed Nagui had been one of the leading painters in Alexandria at the beginning of the twentieth century. But in her own right, Effat had succeeded in creating her own following by painting folk subjects such as icons, charms, pendants, and talismans. Finally, in April 2001, a museum devoted to the work of Effat Nagui and her late husband Saad El Khadem was opened to the public in a villa on Karim Street in Heliopolis, a suburb of Cairo. Effat bequeathed the villa to the Egyptian people with the stipulation that her home be turned into a museum exhibiting her works and those of her husband. They both painted with characteristic folkloric motifs and magical interpretations. El Khadem had been a professor of art education and was familiar with the trades and folkloric genres. One of the themes that is repeated in his work is the inspiration from the Nubian and the pharaonic cultures. Effat was greatly affected by this style of work as well. She produced the captivating works on the Zodiac that became almost a signature of her work, particularly "Scorpio" and "Pisces," two of her best works. There have been many other Egyptian women painters, including Injy Aflaton, Kamel el Telmissani, Taheyya Halim, and Gazibiyya Sirri, who were the main women painters of the 1950s. Aflaton was famous for surrealistic paintings; el Telmissani drew on the ordinary lives of Egyptians for her inspiration; Halim used dark shades of colors to depict animals, landscapes, farms, and people; and Sirri used abstract compositions to emphasize the role of women in society. She was the closest Egyptian painter to the feminist idea in art.

The July 23, 1952 revolution was like a shock wave that washed away all dangling pieces of the art culture not firmly planted in the soul of the Egyptian people and gave them a newfound brand of political art. There had been many attempts to revolutionize Egyptian art prior to the coming of the colonels. However, those attempts had largely been moves by Westerners who sought to transform Egyptian cultural history. Take the case of the "Al Mohawiloun" or "The Essayists" as they were called in 1934. This was a movement led by two non-Egyptians: Jules Levy and Albert Salitel. It failed to galvanize the masses of the Egyptian people, but it did establish the fact that there was a public waiting to discover a connection to the West through the art channel. The Essayists published a journal that was called *Un Effort* and what an effort it was to keep the intellectual focus clear so that the artists would have space to work. It was just a few years later, in 1937, that another group was founded called "The New Eastern Group" in response to the desire to have a statement from the Islamists. They were, after all, in Africa and really southerners but they identified with the East as Easterners as a reaction to the influence of the non-Egyptians in *Un Effort.*

By 1939, a group calling itself simply "Art and Freedom" appeared in the art world and, through their writings and lectures, began to influence the art culture of Egypt in ways that the other groups had not. There was a generation of artists being prepared who would have political commitment but excellent artistic skills. They were led by the likes of George Henein, Ramses Younan, Fouad Kamel, and Kamel el Telmissani. They found surrealism to be one of the best modes for the creation of change in the society. Ramses Younan, for example, expressed a contemplation and surrealist outlook that might be called a "shattered abstract composition" with strange colors and shapes (Gharib 1998, 18). Others such as Fouad Kamel and Salah Taher were convinced that they had to use disturbed compositions to upset the traditional, to announce that they were indeed present in the artistic world. They were rebels against an archaic political situation. Of course, the political establishment arrested and jailed many of these artists.

These artists inspired the movement toward modernity, which the new abstract artists accepted as a part of rebellion. Some, such as Monir Kanaan and Ahmad Fouad Selim, sought to emblazon the Arabic calligraphy in color. Abdul Rahman al Nashar was an impressionist who increasingly became a geometrician. Nevertheless, they inspired the contemporary-art generation— that is, the generation of the revolution itself—which was founded around 1946 by the art teacher Hussein Youssef Amin and the painter Samir Rafe, who had worked with the Art and Freedom movement. Participating in the new movement were people such as Abdul Hadi al Gazzar, Hamed Nada, Ibrahim Massouda, and Maher Ra'ef; in fact, Nada and al Gazzar had started as surrealists seeking a new path for their expression. They were outstanding painters who used mythology, symbolism, and ceremonies to create their works. Some have claimed that Nada's work was happy and merry and that the work of al Gazzar was based on folk themes (Gharib 1998, 19). Clearly these artists were convinced that it was necessary to use the strongest possible artistic methods to break with the archaic characteristics of much Egyptian art.

Exhibitions were the key to success for this group. They were influenced by the developments in the world around Egypt; and although they saw the importance of Egyptian society and its relationship to the contemporary art they were producing, they could not help but be impacted by the political and social climate around them. One of the avenues they used to express their politics was through the exhibitions of paintings of the poor people of the villages and the economically poor regions of Cairo itself. They were on a mission as clearly and as surely as the colonels would soon be on a mission to bring a new dispensation to the country.

Although the contemporary art movement survived during the revolution and continued to exhibit, it would have competition with other groups that had their beginnings about the same time. One was the "Voices of the Artist," founded by the sculptor Gamal el Segeini in 1945. Several transformations happened in this group and it was finally called "Modern Egyptian Art". But the longest lasting of all these contemporary groups was the "Art and Life Society" that was founded by the intellectual Hamed Said in 1946. Said had set a strict discipline for his group, disavowing any political orientation, rejecting European domination of art concepts, and avoiding heated political and social issues (Gharib 1998, 16).

When the revolution occurred, a group of artists initiated a movement to underscore the commitment to national history and events. The 1956 Tri-partite Aggression, as it is called in Egyptian history, the building of the Aswan High Dam, and the June 1967 defeat of Egypt by Israel were all memorialized by the artists. The "Group of Five Artists" formed in 1962 by Reda Zaher, Nabil Wahba, Abdul Hamid al-Dawakhli, Nabil el Hosseini, and Farghali Abdul Hafiz was important in the artistic evolution that occurred during the 1960s. This group was mainly centered in Cairo. Their influence on the generation that followed was significant because they combined the interests of the earlier revolutionary-era artists with a concentration of skills, talents, and imagery.

A "Group of Three Artists" appeared in Alexandria at about the same time, and almost as a response to the Cairo "Group of Five Artists". The "Group of Three" was created in 1965 and included Said al Adawi, Mahmoud Abdallah, and Mustafa Abdul Mo'ti. This group was called an experimental cadre of artists and should not be confused with another "Group of Three" formed in Alexandria in 1969, called "Art and Man," which included Adel el Masri, Farouk Shehata, and Ahmed Azmi. All the artists felt a need to express an Egyptian character to art and culture. It was the "Lovers of Nature and Heritage" group, under the influence of Abdul Qader Mukhtar, that expressed its mission as the affirmation of a particular Egyptian character in fine arts in 1979.

The Egyptian people are proud of their history as well as the massive collections of ancient and contemporary art present in the country. Thus, the discovery, or the rediscovery, of the Kasr el-Eini Musuem of Medical Arts caused a stir in Cairo and its suburbs in 2001. Professor Mahmoud Fawzi el-Manawi, professor of gynecology at the faculty of medicine at Cairo University, has sought to preserve the Kasr el-Eini as a museum to honor the pioneers of modern Egyptian medicine. Originally built as a palace for Ahmed ibn el-Eini in 1447, the building was used as the headquarters for the French Expedition in 1799. It became a part of the Cairo University as a medical school in 1925. It is the perfect setting for the combination of art and history of modern Egypt.

El-Manawi learned in the 1970s that the rare collections of medical papers, drawings, illustrations, and paintings were nearly ruined because of plumbing problems. He was greatly disturbed by this condition and sought to agitate the government officials and anyone who would listen about the need to save the papers. Rescuing the papers stored in the basement of Kasr el-Eini in 1973, el-Manawi found support from then-Minister of Higher Education, Dr. Mofid Shihab, to save the documents. They were infested with insects and some had been damaged. Oil paintings and granite busts had to be restored or cleaned and properly curated.

Soon a team of forty restorationists from the Antiquities Restoration Centre of Cairo University, headed by el-Manawi, began their work. The neglected storage building was transformed into a well-lit, beautiful showcase for the many objects and papers discovered in the basement of the museum. The government spent 2 million Egyptian pounds on the project, but much more needs to be done to bring the items to an international-presentation level.

Among the items on display is a copy of the original *Description de l'Egypte* by Dominique-Vivant Denon and his team of French writers. This copy was supposedly donated to the medical school by Ferdinand de Lesseps. There are also maps of the eighteenth and nineteenth centuries, rare medical books and manuscripts, and busts and paintings of famous medical personalities such as Antoine Bertelemy Clot, founder of the medical school; Theodore Maximilian Bilharz, discoverer of bilharziasis; Ali Pasha Ibrahim, the twentieth-century pioneer of modern Egyptian medicine; Mohammed Olivi Pasha, professor of ophthalmology, who persuaded Princess Fatimah, daughter of Khedive Ismail, to give all her property for the setting up of Cairo University; and Mohammed el-Bakli Pasha, who Egyptianized the Kasr el-Eini medical school.

It is believed that this medical museum is the only one of its kind in the whole of Africa or in southwest Asia. The work done by el-Manawi is remarkable and the Egyptian people bestowed upon him the 2000 State Merit Award for his indefatigable spirit in bringing to the forefront the extensive medical history of the country. In accepting the award, he said, "My efforts are only a small donation to an institution without which none of our professors could have attained such high levels of excellences in the field of medicine" (*Egypt* August 2001, 57). He remains committed to rescuing even more works for display.

GRAPHIC ARTS

Egypt has some of the best graphic artists working in the contemporary art world. They are committed to their art and the strong symbolism they have to draw upon in order to advertise or represent corporations, companies, or governments. Perhaps no group of graphic artists in any country has at its disposal so many varieties of artistic images and themes as the modern Egyptian graphic artist. They are at once the intellectual inheritors of the most monumental civilization in antiquity and at the same time have received the legacy of Islam's most authentically rich and powerful heritage in Africa. Some of the creative designs of the artists harken back to the days of the gods and goddesses of the ancient times, and many of their designs simply

Children making carpets

reflect the infinite variations of Arabic calligraphy. In both cases, the resources and skills of the artists have been used in popular magazines, airline journals, department stores, hotels, and newspapers.

TEXTILES AND FASHION

Many types of weaving exist in Egypt; influences exist from Persia, Turkey and Afghanistan. The country is a nation that has not forgotten its old traditions. In fact, the creative styles of the weavers and carpet makers are grounded in the history and culture of the people. Like the thousands of sculptors who work at the tourist sites, the weavers and carpet makers are seeking to demonstrate their skill and in the process make a living. Very few of the textile makers will deliberately sew or weave clothes into the Western style, although the appetite for Western clothes has not diminished in Egypt since the days of John F. Kennedy. Egyptians are always apologizing for the lack of skilled people in some of the trades, but textiles is not one of them because there is an abundance of talented, trained people who work in this field. Indeed, the carpet schools, often thought of as exploitative, are responsible for creating a vast number of young people who know how to make a living.

Egypt is the fashion capital of the Arab world. Rich princes and princesses

Carpet school

of the Arab emirates and Saudi Arabia arrive in Cairo daily to shop and view the latest in fashions. But it is not the rich sheiks alone who find Cairo fashions attractive and appealing. More and more Egyptians are taking to the shopping malls that are springing up around Cairo and Alexandria to find their own special dresses or outfits. Prices range from very expensive to inexpensive, thus poor people can also afford to shop in the malls. The clothing, mostly made of cotton, in Egypt is well made and reflects the desire on the part of the manufacturers to be able to supply the masses with good-looking ordinary clothes. On the other hand, some of the Giza and Heliopolis shops carry the most expensive fashions to be found on earth (see also the section on clothing in Chapter 5, "Social Customs and Lifestyles").

NOTES

1. This does not mean that the Egyptians were uninfluenced by other cultures. For example, the modern cities of Cairo and Alexandria have many buildings of French, English, and Italian architecture.

2. It should be remembered that many of the artisan skills are mastered by the rural people without the benefit of schools. Most of them are trained by their parents from an early age. One can still find in the small towns of Egypt carpet schools where young people are trained to make carpets for the national and international

markets. In addition, one finds hieroglyphic, jewelry-making, and papyrus-making schools.

3. The government of President Gamal Abdel Nasser sought to bring all Egyptians into the institutional life of the country. Thus, Ahmed Othman, one of the finest artists in modern Egyptian history, was given the position of administering the Faculty of Fine Arts.

4. For a thorough accounting of the artistic developments in contemporary Egypt, see Gharib (1998).

5. A good source for this concrete information is Gharib (1998).

5

Social Customs and Lifestyles

IN ANCIENT TIMES, Egypt was called "the land of the Nile and the sun."[1] Even now these two features dominate the climate of modern Egypt and have a profound influence on the social customs and lifestyles of contemporary Egyptians. Winter is from December to February. During this time the land enjoys brilliant sunshine. Spring is from March to May; summer from June to August; and autumn from September to November. While winter is the season of the clearest skies, owing to the lack of dust and sand in the air, all seasons are pleasant. For instance, summer is never too hot because of the constantly blowing northerly winds. If it is hot during the day—it can get to more than 100 degrees Fahrenheit—it will always be much cooler during the evenings. Most of the year the weather is dry, becoming humid a few days a year during August. In the desert one can see extremely sharp contrast between summer and winter, day and night, temperatures. However, in the Nile Valley the temperatures are unusually stable. One does find contrasts between the two main seasons; but for the most part if it is summer, it is universally hot, and if it is winter, it is less hot but with brilliant sun. One can just about depend on the weather being consistent from day to day. In many respects this is a part of the legacy of stability in Egyptian social customs and lifestyles.

TRAVEL

Travel in Egypt is quite easy and comfortable. The Egyptian people are eager to assist one another as well as foreigners who visit the country. There are many miles of paved highways for automobile and bus travel as well as hundreds of miles of railroad track for train travel. Persons seeking to move between major cities will find several airlines that fly domestic routes. The principal airline is Egypt Air, however, the country supports several smaller airlines as well. In Egypt, the principal industrial and economic cities such as Alexandria, Aswan, Cairo, Hurghada, Luxor, and Port Said are served daily by modern jet aircraft.

Rail travel in Egypt is second to none. The trains are clean and run on time. One can understand that efficiency is built into the system largely by tradition. If the Egyptians have pride in anything it seems to be in the way the railways are run. There is a reason for it. Egypt was the third country in the world to build a railroad when the Cairo–Alexandria line was completed in the nineteenth century. All the modern trains are air conditioned and have dining cars. Normally one can find a train that is a *rukkab* (ordinary; U.S. equivalent of local) as well as an express. The *rukkab* stops at every station, while the express only stops at the most important stations. Thousands of people ride the trains each day and one of the best tourist experiences is taking the train from Cairo to Aswan.

Ownership of Property

Social organization beyond the family is based on ownership of land or other property. Ownership is either public or private. This means that the government of Egypt can and does control the ownership of some large public enterprises such as the post office, railways, roads, ports, airports, and dams. Some of the heavy mining industries are also supported by the government although there is heavy pressure from the international money sector for Egypt to open up even more to Western industrialized capital. All banking and financial institutions remain under the authority of the government. Thus, while individuals and corporations have a large stake in the ownership of property, the government is the major owner of the means of producing wealth in the nation.

There is an active and enthusiastic private sector that operates with the guarantee that private property cannot be expropriated without just compensation. In the tourist trade, there are now international corporations that own some of the hundreds of riverboats. Tourism is becoming one of the greatest areas for capital growth in the country as more young entrepreneurs with Western educations return home from the United States and Europe to set up businesses directly related to the tourism trade. They own companies, hire locals, and engage in international commerce at a very substantial rate. This means that the private sphere has continued to expand even as the

Papyrus store in Cairo

government has tried to hold the reins of major industries so as not to unsettle the economic health of the nation.

Private ownership of farming lands is maintained and protected by the governing authorities, and farms are subject, as buildings are, to the laws of taxation. Under the government of Hosni Mubarak there has been a movement toward more involvement of the masses with control of farms and small businesses. Egypt has recognized the benefit of entrepreneurs, especially in the tourist industry, who are committed to the political and economic goals of the society. There is a growing respect among the state economists for the value of new entrepreneurs. This has brought about a lot of changes in regards to how Egypt is viewed and how it views itself within the continent of Africa, which is seeking to broaden the participation of its people in the democratizing of property.

FARMING

Egypt is a farming country. As one of the three pillars of the Egyptian economy (the others being tourism and oil), Egypt has always made agriculture a key component of its life as a nation. Agriculture was born in the Nile Valley thousands of years ago and has remained one of the noblest of Egyptian occupations.

Farmhouse and farm

Two aspects of farming in Egypt have captured the imagination of the modern person: the use of agricultural implements to assist human labor and the development of farm irrigation. Taken together these aspects of the modern Egyptian society represent a continuing relationship with the past because there seems to be little variation in some of the implements and irrigation methods that were used in the past. Of course, if one were to look at the long history of Egypt, the variation would be obvious. For example, water-lifting devices came late in the development of agriculture, but there have been some shifts in construction and design. The *shaduf*, the so-called counterpoise lift, was created about 1500 B.C.E. but is quite present in contemporary Egypt as is the *sakia* (waterwheel) which did not appear until the fourth century B.C.E.

Agriculture could not exist in Egypt without irrigation because there is not enough rain; therefore, it is necessary to take the water from the Nile and distribute it throughout the farmlands. This has always been the case, so the people are accustomed to creating their own methods of bringing water to their farms. The modern methods are merely evolutions of the old. The Nile is everyone's "rainstorm" and without it there would be nothing but desert in Egypt. If one looks at the beginning of the modern period of Nile River control, in 1843, one can appreciate the fact that the construction of el-Kanater el Khairiya Barrage at the apex of the Delta was a way to raise the level of water upstream and then allow the water to flood the Delta in the low season. Then in 1902, the Aswan Dam was built to further the storage of water. However, the most effective system of water storage and flood maintenance was the building of the Aswan High Dam in 1960. Water is distributed among various canals under a rotation system of watering and closing days whose duration varies depending on the season and the zone.

This healthy supply of water has made Egypt one of the best producers of food in its region of North Africa. Cultivation of lands have been increased more than threefold since the building of the Aswan High Dam. While there has been a steady plan to diversify, the country still has a strong agricultural sector that plays a major role—alongside tourism, the Suez Canal, oil production, and food processing—as a pillar for the economy. Cotton is the primary crop but others—rice, onions, beans, fruits, and oil—contribute to the economy as well.

LIFESTYLES

How do the people of Egypt live day to day? This section will discuss the way Egyptians live and indeed, in some instances, have lived from the earliest of times. The customs of the rural people are quite different from some of those of the urban centers that have increasingly defined the country of Egypt. For example, the middle-class or rich Cairenes have a much different approach to life than the people of Esna who know all of their neighbors and who may come in from the farms each market day to meet relatives. In Cairo, the pace is rather fast. One could get very lost in a city of 18 million people.

Almost all customs in Egypt are related to the Islamic religion or its influence. This means that the followers of the Coptic Christian religion and the Jews have been impacted by the predominance of Islamic culture. Egypt's participation in the Islamic culture does not make it the same as other Islamic societies—in fact, it is quite different in many respects. The people of Egypt see themselves as connected to the African continent and having similarities with other peoples of Africa, particularly Sudan and Libya.

Yet the morning greeting *as salaam alaikum* ("Peace be upon you") and the response *wa laikum salaam* ("and to you") are typically Islamic and are understood by all Egyptians regardless of their background. Thus, to have any real understanding of Egyptian customs one must have some appreciation of the Arabic language inasmuch as the ancient African language—*Mdw Ntr* (the divine words)—and other languages have been swept aside by the historical advance of Arabic.

The Arabic language is quite eloquent in its use of adjectives, adverbs, and names of affection. Thus, Egyptians are very fond of using words such as "dear," "brother," "sister," or appellations of respect for elders, leaders, and persons of high regard. Florid Arabic is considered the best Arabic, and those who have the command of it are deemed eloquent in the use of the language.

WOMEN'S POSITIONS

Advocates of women's rights and privileges have been many. Qasim Amin (1863–1903) appeared as a defender of the rights of women long before independence.

Contrary to popular belief about Egypt, numerous writers have written in support of the liberation of women. However, the most important writer prior to the revolution to address the issue was Amin. His two books— *The Liberation of Women* and *The New Woman*—represented an assault on both Ottoman domination and Western colonialism. *The Liberation of Women* was published in 1899, and *The New Woman* was published in 1900. Both books, which were reprinted in 2000 in one volume, added to the rich corpus of Amin's writings and gave a new orientation to the social customs of the society. He was a member of the Nationalist Reform Movement that challenged the Western intellectuals who attacked the social mores of the Arabic culture.

When Amin wrote these books, Egypt was still under Britain's yoke, although the times were changing and the sentiment for freedom and independence was gaining ground among the Egyptian intellectuals. But how can you advance the move toward independence and representation without taking women along? This was the issue that Amin confronted in his books. He argued, as other African intellectuals would later, that the liberation of women was a prerequisite for the liberation of the society. You could not have men free and women enslaved. In this forward-thinking work, Amin contended that the oppression of women in the home was similar to political oppression. There was a serious philosophical bent to Amin's argument. Since women are the nucleus of the family and the family is the basic unit of society, then to liberate women was to liberate the society. He saw the importance of education for women as the key to the success of any political freedom.

Amin sought to convey to his readers that the Qur'an supported his view. He used the sayings of the Prophet Muhammad as a basis for his ideas on the subject of women's liberation. Amin then discussed how some had misinterpreted the *shari'a* and consequently had mistreated women based on their misinterpretations. He attempted to present a more reasonable rendering of the various works. Furthermore, he argued that societies tended to pass down from one generation to the next ideas and opinions that may be negative for the society. Thus, there were some men who kept women oppressed because that is the way it was done by their fathers and their fathers. Amin resisted this tendency and opposed the integration of this tendency into Islamic faith.

The New Woman openly praised Western ideals. He claimed that women in Europe and North America had a greater status than in Egypt. He also saw value in using the political status of women in those regions as a comparative basis for Egypt.

In many ways Qasim Amin was a revolutionary in that his books express a progressive vision of the role of women in Egyptian society. Indeed, Egyptian feminism was present as early as the 1890s and was promulgated by a man. Thus, the recent emphasis in Egypt on the rights of women has a precedent in the nineteenth-century work of Amin. The work of Amin suggested that the intellectuals interested in the cultural landscape could find enough maneuvering space within the framework of the Qur'an to advance a progressive society. Even as recent as 1999, the government of Hosni Mubarak established the National Council for Women (NCW) with the first lady as its president, to tackle the imbalance in women's representation in the political process. Of the 355 members of the People's Assembly just five are women. The traditional view remains that women should not be in politics because they have other duties such as raising a family and homemaking. Since men are not usually taught to be attuned to the special needs of women, women's needs often go unmet because their voices are not heard. President Mubarak has tried to join the NCW with the United Nations Development Fund to increase female turnout during elections. It should be pointed out, however, that this move comes decades after the reversal by the Egyptian court of a quota rule that existed during the government of Anwar Sadat when 10 percent of all assembly seats had to be held by women. When that law was struck down in 1984, the number of women representatives dropped from thirty-six to five.

ISLAM AND WOMEN

Egyptian women have waged a long struggle for equality. Although they have made great strides in gaining their legal rights, they remain well behind men in both socioeconomic and cultural rights. Nevertheless, the Egyptian government has expressed an interest and commitment to the rise of women in every sector of the society (Brooks, 1995).

Like women in other African societies, Egyptian women have sought to better the lives of their children and themselves by seeking to expand their civil rights. In any Islamic society, this search for new rights for women is fraught with controversy. Egypt is a special case because it has led in the fight for the liberation of women in Islam. When one thinks of Islamic feminism, only a few nations come to mind. Egypt is one of them (Fernea, 1998).

Westerners often think of Egyptian women as powerless, dependent, and passively subordinate to men. Yet this is not an entirely accurate picture of the Egyptian society. Although it is true that women's roles are different from men's, women have increasingly attained recognition as equal citizens of the society. One could easily perpetuate a view of Egyptian women as disempowered since so much of the news one hears or so many of the films one sees about Muslim women are negative. But this view is a disservice to the courageous women who have made enormous advances in the face of male domination and in so doing have made their own contributions to social and cultural change.

Several organizations have helped the women's cause in Egypt. Among them are the Alliance for Arab Women, the Arab Women and Value System, the Arab Women's Solidarity Association, the Egyptian Organization for Human Rights, the Egyptian Women Association, and the National Council for Women. In addition, the government has a department of women's affairs in the Ministry of Social Affairs.

The Issue of the *Hijab*

One area of Islamic life that has come under great scrutiny in the West is Islamic dress (Gole, 1994). Many Westerners believe that the dress of Islamic women is oppressive. In Egypt, many women wear the *hijab* (the scarf as head covering) as a part of their daily dress. However, it should be remembered that millions of Egyptian women also wear Western-style dress. And Egyptian women can often be seen wearing Islamic dress without the veil. Many urban women do not wear the full *hijab*. In fact, Cairo and Alexandria are rather fashionable centers of modern dress.

In Islamic society, dress for women is a symbol of certain religious orthodoxies. In some societies like Iran or the former Taliban-run Afghanistan, men created rules and regulations to control women. Egypt does not have any strict governmental laws regulating women's dress. In fact, even the authoritarian governments of Iran or Afghanistan could only impose their rules in the face of public outcry. Those who stress the importance of Islamic dress for women have argued that they are simply seeking to protect the honor of women and to provide for their dignity (Ahmed, 1992). The Egyptian government has no need for any such rationalization to explain policy. Most of the women in high places in the society, professional or governmental, do not wear veils. Not all Egyptian men, however, approve of this behavior by women.

Those who wear the *hijab* voluntarily are signaling their religious conservatism. If one sees the *hijab* in Cairo or Alexandria, then, it is probably being worn by rural Islamic women or women from other Muslim nations such as the United Arab Emirates. Those Egyptian women who do wear the *hijab* maintain that it allows them to be observant Muslims, it protects them from the lustful eyes of men, it allows them to gain respect among other women, it symbolizes a resistance to a secular society, and it is less expensive than Western clothes, allowing them to get by with fewer outfits.

Egyptian women who favor Western dress tend toward fashions that accentuate their femininity. They therefore favor earrings, necklaces, and other jewelry. Egyptian women who adopt Western fashions are stating their independence, career orientation, desire to be less deferential to men, and self-focus. In contrast, the wearers of the *hijab* are demonstrating their more traditional Muslim orientation, and therefore their greater deference to husbands, family, and belief in the separation of the sexes in public spaces.

Polygamy

Since Egypt is a Muslim nation, polygyny (the practice of a man taking multiple wives) is practiced. According to Islamic doctrine, a man may marry up to four wives. Although most men in Egypt do not have four wives, the very fact that it is possible suggests to Westerners that women are oppressed, especially when they consider that women are restricted to just one spouse.

The practice of polygyny is most often seen in the rural areas and among the less educated. Many rural men believe that multiple wives mean more children and therefore more hands in the fields for sowing and harvesting. However, in urban areas where the cost of living is higher and the agrarian lifestyle is not supported, it is difficult and even foolhardy for a man to have more than one wife. Given Egypt's rapid population growth, the need for money in urban areas is a major concern. With the accelerating modernization of the cities, polygyny will probably continue to attract fewer adherents. Nonetheless, it is a firmly entrenched part of the conservative Islamic tradition, and Muslim men see it as one of the cardinal values of Islam.

Women and the Right to Divorce

Egypt is facing issues found in all modern societies. There are instances of men abandoning their children and families, impoverished women trapped in unemployment without food, and women who are in unproductive and often destructive marriages but cannot escape them without the approval of their husbands. Even if a woman's husband had abandoned her for years, she was not free to remarry because she had not been released from the wayward husband.

In March 2000, Egypt put into practice one of the most far-reaching family law changes in the Arab world: Women were now able to secure a divorce. Some women had chosen not to marry prior to the change in the law because they feared becoming slaves to men. A more equitable justice system made it possible for women to feel a sense of pride and dignity. Now a woman can divorce her husband with or without his consent. A woman can also garnish her husband's paycheck by going to the court and demanding child support. If the man should disappear and the woman cannot find him, she can, with the help of the state, relocate to an apartment and take care of her children.

In the past, for a woman to get a divorce, she had to prove to the court that her husband was a drug addict, beat her, was sterile, or did not support the family. However, in practice what this meant was that a man could get a divorce and the wife could not.

The 2000 reform is a great breakthrough for the society because the civil and criminal codes in Egypt are an amalgam of secular and Islamic law; this is a real change in the way the people live. In 1979, President Anwar Sadat issued a decree that any woman who wanted a divorce because she objected to her husband taking a second wife could get one. However, it was only legal for a few months until a court declared it unconstitutional. Now the new law should give women some more protection. An interesting point of fact: There are more than 1 million divorce cases filed each year, but the judges only grant about 75,000.

WEDDINGS

Egyptians love weddings. In the past most weddings, even high-society weddings, were held in the home. The hosts would often create areas in gardens or on roofs to accommodate the many invited guests. This is not the case anymore. Now everyone wants to have a wedding at one of the newer hotels in Egypt. The weddings are quite expensive and include live musicians and large limousines. To really underscore the fact that the wedding is important, it is necessary to have a belly dancer. In his book *Whatever Happened to the Egyptians?* (1995, p. 24), Galal Amin wrote that when he was growing up in Egypt, weddings were more traditional. There were no belly dancers, no buying of the wedding dress, and no coiffeur. These accoutrements are

Belly dancer

now quite standard in middle-class weddings in Egypt. They add considerable expense to the costs of the wedding.

The word for wedding in Arabic is *farah*, which carries with it the meaning
of "joy" and "merriment." Before the 1952 Revolution, Egyptians could not
have conceived of having a wedding without neighbors and friends from the
community involved in the activities. While the revolution did not cause the
changes in the way the *farah* was carried out, it brought about new ideas,
innovations, and novel expressions of culture. By the 1970s the middle class
had already begun to have weddings in large hotels, although the number of
hotels was limited because tourism had not yet become such a major player
in the recreational industry. Nevertheless, the Egyptian idea of a great wedding was being defined by the big bashes at the Mena House and other hotels.

Whatever the traditions had been, new rites and rituals developed as more
and more weddings took place at hotels. However, there were certain activities that could not be performed at high-priced hotels. For example, the
"celebratory ululations of women, the *zaghruta*, are scarcely heard, if at all,
at these hotel parties" (Amin 1995, 111). It is surmised that many of the
wedding parties at hotels are attended by invited guests who think of the
zaghruta as beneath them; but it may be more a matter of hotel protocol.
Having women perform the high-pitched shrill in the hotel ballrooms might
be seen as out of place in a modern hotel. But what about the practice of

sharing *milabbis* (sugar-coated almonds) or the drinking of *sharbat* (a drink made from diluted syrup)? At hotel wedding parties the sharing of *milabbis* has often been forgotten as has been the drinking of *sharbat*. These are small changes in the wedding celebrations, even though Egyptian culture suggests that sweet foods should be associated with good times. The sweeter the food, the better the celebration. Many Egyptians refer to something that is rare such as a fruit. Thus, people go to great lengths to add sweets to their celebrations.

According to Amin, "the splendor of the *milabbis* container was one of the principal means by which the upper classes distinguished themselves from the lower. In hotel weddings, however, if the *milabbis* features at all, it makes an embarrassed appearance as if the remnant of a custom on its way to extinction" (ibid.). The *sharbat* is often mixed with fruit juices to please tastes of more Westerners, who often attend high-society weddings.

As with most weddings, there is tremendous pressure on the families. However, hotel managers add even more tension because of certain non-traditional requirements. For example, few hotels allow children at weddings, and the invited guests are often told on their invitations not to bring children.

The wedding party is usually surrounded by music—either live or recorded—which is highly amplified, making it almost impossible for guests to converse. However, this is considered a good thing because Egyptians feel that it is quite Egyptian to have loud music playing in the background at a party. It is also quite Egyptian to have a good time at a wedding.

FOODS

Egyptian food is well-known in the Arab world and is becoming more popular in the West, as evidenced by the many Middle Eastern/Mediterranean restaurants and the offering of Middle Eastern/Mediterranean food in grocery stores. The idea of "Middle Eastern" foods is interesting because there is rarely a country identified with it, most people assume that it represents the creation of the Mediterranean basin, with the exception of the Greeks since the Greeks have their own type of food. To a large degree one does see influences from different countries on Egyptian foods, but the main portion of Egypt's contribution to world cuisine is Egyptian. This is not to say that others have not borrowed heavily from Egypt, as the world has for thousands of years, to provide their own people with richness and variety.

There is not much regional variation to the foods of Egypt, and so it is possible to list a few of them that have gained national and international prominence. *Kebab* is skewered mutton pieces, now typically interspersed with beef or chicken, grilled over charcoal and garnished with parsley. The Egyptians also skewer and grill pigeons and serve them in kebab restaurants. *Hamam fil tagen* is pigeons buried in pilaf rice, mixed with cream, and placed in a *tagen* (clay pot) and baked in an oven. *Dulmah* or *mahshi* is hollowed-out tomatoes, eggplants, green peppers, or squash that are stuffed with rice mixed with minced meat, parsley, and spices. It is served with yogurt. *Messaka* is sliced eggplant cooked in oil and tomato sauce and topped with minced meat and pine kernels. *Bamia* (okra) is cooked in tomato sauce and beef broth. It is usually tried with paprika and lemon juice added. *Bamia nashfa* is crushed dried okra cooked with pieces of mutton in a brown hot sauce. *Ruz bel kharta* is a mound of rice topped with chicken livers, raisins, pine kernels, and nuts and is usually served with turkey or chicken cutlets.

Some of the vegetables grown in Egypt are as follows:

Tomato, *Uta*	Eggplant, *Betengan*
Turnip, *Left*	Garlic, *Tom*
Artichoke, *Kharshuf*	Haricot beans, *Lubyia*
Cabbage, *Koronb*	Lettuce, *Khas*
Carrot, *Gazar*	Green Pepper, *Felfel*
Celery, *Karafs*	Parsley, *Ba'dunis*
Cauliflower, *Arnabit*	Potato, *Batatis*
Chard, *Sala*	Raddish, *Fegle*
Cucumber, *Khiar*	Spinach, *Sabanekh*
Peas, *Besella*	

Many modern Egyptians prepare foods in the same way that it has been prepared for generations. It is not uncommon to see outdoor ovens at which women sit for hours baking bread as their grandmothers did. Perhaps this is why Egyptian food has gained a wide reputation for being excellent. The Egyptian women are among the best bakers in the world, and the various foods of the society are highly seasoned and spiced as befitting a nation with so many different cultural strands.

Food is important to Egyptians during a long day because they rise early and stay up late into the night. The typical day will begin at 6:00 A.M. and end about 9:00 P.M. However, some urban dwellers' days will be even longer because they will spend hours fraternizing with friends and celebrating at parties. In Cairo, some nightclubs are open all night. This is not the case in rural areas, however, because strict, conservative Islam prevents such behavior. By the end of the day, a person has been exposed to foods and drinks reflective of the hospitality that is legendary among the Egyptians.

Egyptian farmers send their customers an enormous variety of fresh vegetables, fruits, fish, and meats. No one need ever worry about the variety of food an Egyptian will prepare. Most tables will have a combination of fruits, breads, and meats. The idea is to give the person as much choice as necessary to satisfy hunger and desire.

There are two main traditions in Egyptian foods: African and Arabic. African cuisine is seen in the many uses made of fish, cattle, wild game, and tropical fruits and plants. This is a continuing foundation for much of Egyptian cuisine. However, the Arabic cuisine that has come to dominate Egyptian food is related to what has been called "tent cookery," with a base of dates and rice—transportable foods. In addition, the inclusion of lamb, goat, and camel in the cuisine is directly related to the ambulatory nature of the animals.

Culinary responsibilities are gender specific in the sense that one almost never sees a man baking or taking on the majority of the cooking. It is considered a woman's job, and many wives believe that if they are unable to cook, their husbands will leave them. The idea, therefore, is for a young girl to watch her mother so that she will master the techniques of preparing the recipes that have been handed down from generation to generation. One can easily see young girls of six or seven years old assisting their mothers with the cooking chores. By the time a girl is fifteen she should be an expert at making the major dishes of the culture. Of course, city girls are quite different from rural girls, and they do not have the same pressures on them to excel at culinary duties.

Rural Egyptian cooking is centered around the cooking hearth. Stones serve as a tripod with a pot set over burning firewood in an open space. All kitchens have facilities suitable for boiling, frying, roasting, grilling, steaming, and baking. The Egyptian oven is a separate structure from the hearth, normally made of clay as it would be in Nigeria or Sudan or other African nations.

As with other things, Egyptian food has numerous influences from other countries in Africa as well as Asia. The acquisition of spices and recipes from the various peoples who make up the society has added to the luxuriant meals that are served in the country. The food is highly appreciated for its reliance on natural ingredients and the ease with which it is digested. This does not mean that the food is monotonous or dull; rather, it is that Egyptians, who prefer their own foods to any other, have mastered the art of spicing their locally grown vegetables and meats to make them distinctive and inviting.

Custom and tradition are always at the front door of an Egyptian home.

So entering a home brings with it special joys and rituals that must be practiced and honored as they have been for hundreds of years. The Egyptian host is a creature of tradition. One cannot escape the customs even as a Westerner. An Egyptian is not expected to resist but, instead, to understand the fundamentals of good etiquette.

Futoor (breakfast) is an important meal. It usually consists of more than one of the following items: *ful-medames* (baked beans), *gebna beida* (soft white cheese), eggs and *pastorami* (cured beef), *halawa* (sweet sesame cake), jam or honey, and *chai* (tea) or *ahwa* (coffee). Breakfast dishes vary from family to family; many use yogurt as a base. A family will usually begin the morning with *chai* and coffee. One can have a type of Arabic bread, often called *pita* or *shammy*, with any type of meat—except pork—or a dip. Some families eat *gebna beida* in an *ejje* (omelette), which also includes various vegetables, and drink milk for breakfast. Others eat a type of slow-cooked mash of brown fava beans and red lentils called *foul*. Most of these foods are prepared the day of serving, although some of them are previously prepared and kept for the morning meal.

Although breakfast is an important meal, the Egyptian family goes all out for the evening meal that might start as early as 4:00 P.M. or as late as 8:00 P.M. It is here where one sees the incredible array of spices, meats, and cheeses displayed in a dazzling fashion by the cooks. Most people in the world have become familiar with many of the foods used in the Egyptian home or, at least, know something about the preparation of those meals. For example, who is not familiar with the *kebab* (skewered chunks of meat or fish cooked over charcoal) or hummus (a type of puree of chickpeas), *tahina* (lemon and garlic served with a dip), *falafel* (a deep-fried patty filled with spiced ground chickpeas), or *baklava* (a layered pastry filled with nuts and honey-lemon syrup, usually cut into triangles).

Fast-Food Industry

The fast-food industry (mostly American corporations) has invaded the major cities of Egypt—Cairo, Alexandria, and Luxor; one does not find fast-food outlets in the smaller towns. Kentucky Fried Chicken, McDonald's, Wimpy's, Pizza Hut, and Burger King are extremely popular in the Cairo metropolitan area, particularly in the Giza and Heliopolis suburbs. Traditionalists have complained about the invasion of fast food, but the demands of urban dwellers for quickly prepared foods, especially for the lunch hour, have gained immense popularity since the 1980s. However, it is unlikely that the traditional *kebab* and *kofta*—lamb chops, lamb shank, grilled and stuffed pigeon, and grilled chicken—restaurants will be replaced by the American and European upstarts. In most parts of the nation, the people have never heard of Burger King or McDonald's; they carry out their daily quest to satisfy their food desire with the same regularity as their foremothers and forefathers did.

The people of Aswan and Luxor, although heavily influenced by the tourist industry, have managed to stay inside their homes and inside their culture without being too much influenced by the habits of the Americans and Europeans. This is obviously due to the strength of the Islamic culture in the country.

Other Foods

Snacks are not a regular part of the Egyptian's culture yet they are becoming increasingly popular with the advent of the fast-food culture. Therefore, many people have taken to peanuts (which they call groundnuts), pineapples, mangos, bananas, and oranges for snacks. This is to be expected since the country is abundantly rich in terms of agricultural resources, particularly fruits and nuts. One can often find vendors selling foods on the streets, including various rice-based products, nuts, plantains, and kebabs.

Egyptians eat a lot of vegetables. They are found in such abundance that some families subsist on vegetables and fish, never eating meat. The price of vegetables and fish depends on the ingenuity of the family. The Nile River provides a great store of fish for the industrious family and the earth gives up its bounty quite readily if the family is willing to work.

BEVERAGES

Egypt has many popular drinks. Tea is a favorite of the middle classes, but the most popular drink in Egypt is by far coffee, which is believed by Egyptians to have developed and been perfected in their country. Egyptian coffee is very thick and aromatic.

Upon entering an Egyptian home, a visitor is immediately met by the host offering a cup of mint tea or a freshly brewed cup of coffee—this is an age old custom practiced for both social and business occasions. Declining this "gift" is regarded as uncivilized and disrespectful of one's host. However, it is perfectly acceptable to take just a sip and set the rest aside. The tradition originates from the past when people would travel for many miles, often in the hot sun or under heavy rains (certainly not in Egypt, though). Once they arrived at their destination, the host would offer them water or tea before any business or socializing would take place. The offer of the tea, coffee, or water is not ritualized in Egypt among all classes of people. Those who enter the portals of the house must know what the customs are and then respond appropriately.

Egyptian men often meet at restaurants and cafés and sit for hours smoking tobacco from water pipes and sipping the Turkish-style coffee. Drinking coffee is a national tradition. Local coffeehouses—much like men-only clubs in the West—still cater to men who come to drink coffee and converse about politics, sports, and women. The coffee is made from finely powdered beans that are brewed in a small iron pot. When the water begins to boil, the coffee grounds float to the surface in a dark foam. It is then poured from the pot into a demitasse. The heavier grounds stick to the bottom and the lighter ones create the foam in the cup. This is the mark of a perfectly brewed cup of *ahwa*. One quickly finds that the Egyptians sip coffee carefully to avoid the heavier grounds at the bottom of the cup. When the last of the coffee is finished, the cup is turned upside allowing the dregs to form a pattern that can be read by the coffee drinker. Supposedly the interpretation of the dregs should bring good conversation to the participants.

A good strong cup of coffee in the home is thought to bring good luck to one who drinks with a friend and reads the dregs at the bottom of the cup. Of course, some can never complete the cup because of the strength of the coffee and so never have a chance to read the dregs. Many coffee drinkers refer to the taste as tart; but the taste of Egyptian coffee really depends on the mixture of the beans used in the grind. The larger the percentage of Arabica, the sweeter and more chocolate the flavor. The coffee comes in several versions. *Ahwa sada* is very black, *ahwa ariha* is lightly sweetened, *ahwa mazboot* is moderately sweetened, and *ahwaziyada* is very sweet. Coffee and conversation are acceptable reasons to spend time at a café, especially in Cairo and Alexandria.

Another popular drink, especially in Aswan, is *karkaday*, which is made from the hibiscus plant. Its rich taste, with the fragrance of the flower, is a favorite when the weather is hot (which is most of the time) in Upper Egypt. Innovators often add spices to the drink, but most Egyptians like it in its natural, red form. Much like the ubiquitous American cola drinks, *karkaday* is enjoyed by most Egyptians. There may be a few people who refuse to drink it or say they do not like it, but most Egyptians consider the *karkaday* one of their favorite beverages.

Bottled water is popular with tourists in the country. It is available in both small and large bottles and can be found on most of the streets near tourist attractions. The Egyptian water system is mostly safe in the urban areas; the drinking water meets the standards of most nations on the African continent.

Fresh fruit drinks are also available throughout the country. Shopkeepers blend the whole fruit and small amounts of sugar ice or sugar water and then strain this mash into glasses. Among the fruit drinks that are popular with the masses of Egyptians are *manga* (mango), *farawla* (strawberry), *mohz* (banana), and *burtu'aan* (orange). One can also find fruit juices mixed with vegetable juices, especially *khiyar* (cucumber), *tamaatim* (tomato), and *gazar* (carrot). Combination drinks such as *nuss wa nuss* (carrots and orange) and *mohz bi-laban* (bananas and milk) are also easily found in shops. *Asir lamoon*, a common type of lemonade, is very strong and sweet. It is found everywhere in the country as well.

There are many American and European drinks in Egypt, which can be found in almost all stores. The popular brands of Western drinks are Pepsi, Seven-Up, Schweppes, Fanta, and Coca-Cola. When you purchase a soda from a street vendor, it is expected that you will drink it on the spot and return the bottle to the vendor.

Egypt is a Muslim country and devout Muslims refrain from drinking alcohol. However, one can find alcoholic beverages behind closed doors in bars, restaurants, and some grocery stores. The local beer is called "Stella" and is quite popular among the working class and the upwardly mobile. "Zibib" is a local alcoholic beverage that is a kind of Egyptian *ouzo*, after the Greek drink of that name.

FAMILY STRUCTURE

Responsibilities in an Egyptian family are dependent on gender and age. The pivotal person is the father, who in the Islamic tradition is the person responsible for providing for the needs of the family. The mother raises the children and maintains the home. However, the modern Egyptian family is changing and now one can see husbands and wives sharing in the responsibilities of raising the family and providing for the children. In some instances, the household chores may be taken care of by domestic workers. The fact that men and women are sharing in some decisions is not to be taken as a universal behavior in Egypt. It is fundamentally an urban experience that would not be tolerated in the more conservative rural communities.

Sons and daughters are given their duties according to age. Sons are taught how to be protectors of their sisters. Sons are also supposed to help the father with his duties inside and outside of the house. Whatever the father's role is, the son's role is to be supportive. A male child becomes the eyes and ears of his father. Daughters are given the role of being the emotional support of the family. They learn from their mother how to make people comfortable, take care of the men, and become a good homemaker.

Education has created new ways of approaching the family. The husband and wife are both allowed and encouraged to attend college. Part of the

Celebrating a child in Aswan

contemporary change in the gender responsibilities and roles is due to education. Some things, however, do not change. One son is still expected to remain at home to take care of the parents. Girls are still expected to learn how to take care of the home. A woman who marries an Egyptian man will usually not take his name. However the role of women is quite clearly defined in the customs of Egypt. A woman lives at her family house until she is married. Once she is married she is expected to move to the home of her husband. It is almost unheard of for a man to move to his wife's home.

Over the past twenty years, changes have occurred in urban Egyptian society in the way women are viewed and the way they view themselves. A young woman might hold a 10 to 5 job, attend graduate courses at the university, cook and clean at home for her husband, drive through the crowded streets of Cairo or Alexandria to a shopping center, and return home in time to go with her husband to a wedding reception at one of the beautiful Cairo hotels. The changes for women have been meaningful for the society because women now work in government or business alongside men, teach in colleges and universities, and hold positions in banking and social services. Thus, the relationship with men has changed for women, and they now exhibit greater self-confidence and independence.

One example of the change that might confuse an uninformed onlooker is the spread of the *hijab* (the covering for the hair that is now used by many middle-class women). Since the *hijab* is so common among women now, it could be assumed that it reflects a new provincialism; however, Galal Amin believes that the wearing of the *hijab* "represents a trend toward greater movement of previously secluded women into the outside world" (2000, 84). So it is not confinement or fanaticism that causes the wearing of the *hijab*, but evidence of more openness and freedom among women in the society.

However, the changing status of women is not approved by all Egyptian society. There still remains a group of men who believe that the changing conditions in the lives of women have created restless children, instability in marriages, and more family disputes. Thus, while it is true that women have come a long way, they still have a long way to go to full equality.

NAMING OF CHILDREN

The naming of children follows the religious tradition. Therefore, most names are Muslim. Most children receive names after individuals from the Qur'an or from Islamic history. Boys and girls are happy to have names that relate to the family of the Prophet Muhammad. The most popular name in Egypt is the most popular name in the world for males: Muhammad.

BIRTHDAY CELEBRATIONS

The urban middle and upper classes celebrate their children's birthdays with parties to which other children are invited to share in food and games. It is rare for the birthdays of children in the rural areas to be celebrated with as much fanfare. Occasionally the wealthy hold birthday celebrations at major hotels with Western dance music playing in the background. The celebration of birthdays, while traditional in Egypt, has taken on some aspects of the West. For some urban birthday parties, invitations are often sent and guests bring gifts.

SOCIAL BEHAVIOR

Egyptians normally behave conservatively in public. They do not display affection between the sexes. Egyptians are private people and believe that one should keep his or her personal affections private and behind closed doors. When men are around women in public, they usually do not exhibit raucous laughter or any kind of behavior that will seem uncontrolled; however, in private they may be quite boisterous. Arguments between friends and spouses are almost never made public; the idea is to guarantee that no one else is aware of a problem.

When a man meets a woman, he never greets her with a kiss. If the woman extends her hand, he may shake it, but, otherwise, greeting her with words is appropriate and expected. Furthermore, a man never comments to another man about the beauty of his wife. These are conventions that help to maintain the Egyptian sense of privacy in personal matters. It is not another man's place to comment on a man's wife's beauty; to do so is to meddle.

Privacy is an important aspect of Egyptian culture. Even houses are built with solid walls to ensure privacy from the street traffic and neighbors. People who visit relatives or friends stand at the front door in such a way as not to look into the person's house; and they do not enter until the host invites them in with an outstretched palm-up right hand.

CUSTOMARY BEHAVIORS

The patriarchal family is the basic unit in the society. It is based on Islamic morality and religion and the traditions of the society are embedded in children at a very early age. Safeguards to the family are provided in the forms of social insurance for those who are ill, handicapped, or disabled; but women remain undereducated and relegated to the background in most rural families. There is change underway in Egypt, however, as the large cosmopolitan population of Cairo is driving the rest of the society toward a more liberal policy regarding women. Nevertheless, the overwhelmingly patriarchal nature of the Egyptian family remains an essential fact of life.

There are a number of customary duties that all Egyptians must observe. One of the most important is looking after someone who is ill. When someone gets ill, the neighbors will go to the house to greet the person and will provide support, food, and comfort. This also happens when the person is in the hospital. A visitor might bring fruits, nuts, chocolates, and coffee to the sick person. Older relatives of the sick person must prepare refreshments for those who are visiting the sick. In such a way there is a general attitude of hospitality.

The same type of generosity and hospitality is shown when two people marry or have a baby. Friends and relatives bring gifts of money or something useful for the house. When a baby is born, the relatives and neighbors congratulate the woman and present her with gifts. Most mothers remain in the family house for forty days after the birth of the baby. She will be taken care of by her mother and sisters. The baby will be held, changed, and fed by all of the women in the house. Since the Egyptian culture is very detail-oriented, the neighbors and relatives must observe the social rules of caring, generosity, and respect. These values are actually carried out by the kinds of actions that people take.

Arabic as a language has a number of phrases that people use to demonstrate their respect and care. For example, when visiting a sick person, one may say, *Maa Teshoof Sharr, Afer Waafia In Shaa Allah* (I pray that you don't see harm, and by God's will it will be added points to you with Allah and you will be cured). When someone is returning from a long trip, the neighbor may say, *Al Hamdo Lillah Ala Al Salamah*, (I thank Allah for bringing you back safe). When visiting someone who has a new baby, *Yetrabba Be Ezz-ekum. Waa Allah Yajaluhoh Min El Thorriah Al Salehah* (May he be raised in your goodness and may Allah make him be a good son). When visiting someone who is getting married, one would say, *Mabrook* (Congratulations).

CLOTHING

Men in Egypt typically wear the *galabea* (a long-sleeved one-piece dress that covers the whole body). This garment comes in several colors; however, most men wear white or light blue. One can also find them in gray, brown, green, and black. The black is usually reserved for formal occasions or for funerals. The *galabea* is an airy garment, made so to allow the air to circulate and keep the body cool during the hot summer days. The multitude of white cotton dressed men coming down a Cairo street reminds one of a low cloud moving in slow motion. Normally the men who wear the *galabea* also wear the three-piece head cover that consists of a small cap worn directly on the head, a large piece of fabric (usually wool) that is a scarflike wrapping that covers the cap, and a large band that holds the entire headpiece in place.

NOTE

1. When Herodotus visited Egypt in the fifth century B.C.E., he observed that the sun and the Nile River were two elements largely responsible for the country of Egypt itself. Since the time of Herodotus, the Egyptians have always recognized the special favor they received from the constant sun and the perpetual river.

6

The Media and Cinema

ARABIC is the official language of Egypt, although English and, to a lesser degree French, are used frequently. Egyptian Arabic has become the dominant form of Arabic in the world because of its widespread use in magazines, television, and cinema. People in other parts of the Islamic world tend to defer to the Egyptian style of Arabic largely because they are more familiar with the Egyptian media and cinema than they are with the media of other countries. With the presence of the powerful news channel Al-Jazeera in Qatar, there will be some competition to the overwhelming reach of the Egyptian media. Nevertheless, what is clear from the first few years of Al-Jazeera is the fact that even the spoken Arabic of the news channel takes on many of the Egyptian forms. Thus, Egypt remains a dominant influence through the media in the Arabic-speaking world.

THE INFLUENCE OF POPULAR CULTURE

Despite its antiquity, Egypt is greatly influenced by contemporary popular culture. Ordinary people, as well as members of the upper classes, often use phrases and terms from television stars and entertainers in their conversation. Just as in previous times when the language of poets entered the conversation and customs of the people who listened to them, now the words of the movie actors or television actors have become the phrases by which people demonstrate their modernity. In many ways this particular cultural style of borrowing from the media is suited to the Egyptian personality and culture. Egyptians are fond of poetic expressions and repartee that come from the cinema or performing arts. There is a strong interest in subjects and themes that re-create the fundamental vision of an Islamic society but there is also a strand in the society that looks to popular culture as the way to modernity. The person who is able to speak or hold a conversation and at the same time refer to something that has been on the television or in a popular movie is considered quite contemporary because it shows that you are in touch with the present.

The term "popular culture" cannot be translated adequately in Arabic. The closest expression, *Al-thaqafa al-sha'biyya*, refers to folklore, quaint speech mannerisms, and festivals, and so does not really convey the same thing as the English term "popular culture."[1]

Mass culture is considered the province of the nonintellectual, the ignorant. Many people see the traditional cultures as backward. This is not unlike the situation in many African countries where the cultures of the ancestors are looked upon as not functional in the modern world. Yet the Egyptian people recognize a didactic tendency in the culture that always brings the artist back to the authentic pathways of the traditional culture. One could expand, elaborate in ways, and perhaps modify, but it must all be done in accordance with the traditional standards.

A prominent literary critic once asked the question, "Is the culture of the Egyptian countryside truly suitable today to be the raw material for the civilization of the 20th century?" (Awad 1969, 6). Awad puzzled that "the bourgeoisie of Cairo is trying to save the bourgeoisie of the provinces from the coarse hell of the countryside lurking all about them like a ghoul waiting to ambush them and swallow them up" (1969, p. 6). Of course, the severe attack that Awad leveled against the rural peasants could have been more bitter had he attacked the urban peasants. They, too, did not live the modern life although they lived so close to modernity. What was true of the country people was also true of the urban peasants.

Modern culture has undergone a reevaluation since the time of the 1967 war when Egypt was humbled by the Israeli army. This defeat had a defining character to it for the Egyptian people. It meant a questioning of everything, including the popular culture and its use in the development of the nation. By 1973, the end of a transition period away from the old form of imitating the West culturally to a new, bolder self-assertion of Egyptian culture, the society had found respectability again on the battlefield. It had also found itself looking to its own cultural roots in a nationalistic swing to modernity.

The *Infitah* (open-door economic policy coming after 1973) accelerated the path toward modernity. Egyptians, like many African and Arabic nations, felt an obligation to demonstrate their understanding and appreciation of the modern world. Egypt was bent on being not just a maker of the ancient world, but a figure in the modern construction of history as well.

There is no way that the Egyptian society, with its natural historical heritage, could abandon completely its past. In the sense that it is tied to its past, Egypt is different from many countries that want to abandon their pasts. For the Egyptians, modernity is best defined in terms that emphasize continuity, not discontinuity. This is a rational, logical approach to modernity. In the minds of the intellectuals, media and cinema would serve as twin engines to bring the nation into the modern world.

However, Egypt, perhaps, of all Arabic cultures finds itself torn between the desire to defend the classical language and to demonstrate the flexibility in the popular language through the media and cinema. There are two streams of communication going on all the time: the classical written language and the spoken, mediated language of television shows. The Egyptian people are a practical lot, and they respond to both the classical and the popular language. In the end, they will probably make further inroads into the nature of the classical language since language by nature grows and increases in complexity with age and time.

Slang expressions come from popular theater, film, and television and can have an impact on the way younger Egyptians communicate. To say "she has *al-timsaha*" (which literally means "crocodile") is to speak of someone's material achievements. Just as this expression has developed out of the material conditions and responses of the people to cultural artifacts, other linguistic terms will certainly appear as the people speak the language of the popular culture.

THE MEDIA

Television

Television has become a criterion for modernity in most societies. Egypt is no different. This is not to say that the rise of television in Egypt has been without its critics. There are those who applaud the presence of television but decry its use in Egypt. The problems are numerous as seen by critical viewers. Many members of the government recognized that something had to be done to improve the condition of television. In 2001, Mervat Ragab was named chairwoman of television in Egypt. She was asked to restore the Egyptian television to its "past glories."

Broadcasting began in Egypt as early as 1928 with radio. When television was added in the 1940s, ERTV (Egyptian Radio and Television) became the first company of its kind on the African continent. The Egyptian Television Organization was founded in 1960, and Middle East Radio was founded in 1964. These remain the major television organizations in the country.

There are several issues that confront Egyptian television. First, unlike most democratic societies, there is little investigative reporting. Second, there does not seem to be a master plan for television programming that precisely states its mission in Egypt. Third, critics believe that television programming in Egypt needs to be revamped.

All of these problems have been set out by Mamdouh el-Dakhakhni in an article (2001, 22).[2] His contention is that the lack of hard news on Egyptian television means that the viewers do not learn much about what is going on in the world. The most popular news programming in the Arabic speaking world comes from Al-Jazeera, a broadcast television station based in the small emirate of Qatar. Soon after the attack on the World Trade Center and the Pentagon on September 11, 2001, Al-Jazeera began broadcasting, directly to the Arabic world, the results of the American bombardment of Afghanistan. Several times Al-Jazeera correspondents were able to gain access to news that the large Western news services, such as the BBC and CNN, were not able to secure. In Egypt, Al-Jazeera became the authoritative source of information about "America's War on Terrorism." Several times in late 2001, Al-Jazeera was able to gain interviews with Mullah Omar and Osama bin Laden when Western journalists could not find them. Egyptian television has not been able to break out of the mold of following local politicians around as if they are reporting on what is going on in the world. Investigative reporting is lacking.

The three main channels of Egyptian television imitate one another. There is hardly any difference between them when it comes to programming. Viewers often complain that there is no variety and little diversity. One channel could quite easily specialize in presenting the personal stories of ordinary Egyptians such as the Copts, the Bedouins, or the Nubians; this would be an education for the country's viewers. Another idea would be to cover the news of other countries in Africa, and if not the entire continent, certainly the news in Libya and Sudan; this, too, would lead to an informed population. As it is now, each of the three main channels plays it safe by spending their time doing what they believe to be acceptable politically. The ten or so satellite channels are too many to be followed regularly and many adults do not like to leave those channels, if they can afford satellite, to their children. However, they would like to have interesting and informative programming.

In El-Dakhakhni's opinion "Egyptian TV is very noisy and each program has an unnecessarily long preamble with blaring music, flashing pictures and long lists of names which serve little purpose (2001, 23).[3] Anyone who has watched Egyptian television knows exactly what he is talking about. Almost all programs have long introductions that really take away time from the programs themselves. In some societies credits run quickly and silently at the end of the program. It may, however, be a part of the Egyptian culture that could be modified rather than eliminated.

In addition to these issues, El-Dakhakhni finds another problem with the way television programs are structured. He believes that scriptwriters are not using all of the possibilities they have available to devise stories that are substantive. There is nothing of the hero who has both good and bad qualities in Egyptian drama; there are only characters who are "invariably either crooks, womanizers, wheeler-dealers or drug traffickers" (ibid.).

Perhaps what El-Dakhakhni wanted to do was inform the new chairwoman of television that all eyes would be on her as she tried to reform the industry. Furthermore, since Egyptians are influenced by television in terms of behavior and dress, it would be in the interest of the country for programming to be taken more seriously. In fact, El-Dakhakhni was encouraged by the possibility that television could bring about a salutary change in the behavioral patterns of society. It is possible that the late 1980s—the era of "The White Flag"—was the period of "past glories" that the government officers were referring to when they appointed Mervat Ragab.

"The White Flag" was an Egyptian television serial that first aired on December 5, 1989. The powerful opening that shoved serene shots of the Mediterranean coast—a windswept corniche near Alexandria—was broken by cannon bombardment and a bulldozer razing an area. A female voice opens the first speaking scene with "Excuse me. This isn't a new world war. It's Fadda." A sixty-year-old woman yells, "Hammo, boy! The crocodile, let's go!"

The character Fadda al-Madawi would enter the Egyptian imagination for the next fifteen nights as few other characters had ever done. Her words would become part of the popular culture, and ordinary citizens on the streets of Cairo and Alexandria would take the conversation of "The White Flag" to the coffeehouses. The Mercedes Benz 300—the longer, lower, costlier model—was the *al-timsaha*, crocodile. A lesser version of the German car was called the *khanzira* (that is, pig) because it is boxier, less flashy, and less expensive than the crocodile. In Egyptian slang, the newer Mercedes with a raised rear end is called something like the backside of a chicken, *zalamukka*.

What was most telling to the critics about this show was that the apparent vileness of some of the scenes—nothing of course approaching what one watches in the West—was a tremendous success. Fadda was a person who used low-class Arabic and unmistakably gave the common, everyday person in the street someone with whom to identify.

According to one observer, "the use of the crocodile catchphrase was largely a joke. A young male friend living in a poor quarter of Cairo left the house calling to his brother Muhammad, *'Walah Hammo! Al-shanta, yalla'* (Hammo, boy—the bag, let's go!). There would have been no point in him or thousands of others impersonating Fadda if the joke had not touched on something real—the knowledge that someone who talked like Fadda al-Madawi could never legally acquire the means to buy a *timsaha*—but a joke implies ambiguity."[4] What the observer understood was the fact that Egyptians saw so many people driving Mercedes that Fadda's words had meaning. How could a poor, hardworking person, who spoke like Fadda, obtain a Mercedes without being a criminal? In fact, there had to be some form of greed, vulgarity, borderline criminality, and guile to allow a person such as Fadda to succeed. In time, the name Fadda became synonymous with being pushy, vile, and vulgar; it is also used to indicate someone with no class.

Egyptians responded to "The White Flag" in a national outpouring of discussion, debate, and evaluation. Some people have viewed such shows as an attack on the divisions between the rich and the poor. A common complaint was that Egypt had become a country of money. Yet people rallied to the public discussions of the show to express their support for the issues that were revealed in the serial. Middle-class men and women crowded halls to discuss the power of money in the society. Fadda was considered the evil character and Dr. Mufid, the opposing character, a much better person.

The director of the serial, Muhammad Fadil, achieved super status by constructing a drama that revealed the extremes of good and evil. Fadil said that the reason he chose a woman to play the evil character was to heighten the sense of good and evil. Money plays such a major role in the life of Cairo, but this is no different from other societies. However, in a city of 18 million, where one might count ten Mercedes—each costing more than $50,000— within five minutes in downtown Cairo or Heliopolis, and yet most workers earn less than $20,000 a month, the division between rich and poor is brutal.

NEWSPAPERS

The presence of a European printing press on the African continent dates back to 1794 in Freetown, Sierra Leone. As soon as the press arrived from London, a French raiding party came ashore and destroyed it, sacked the city, raped the women, and slaughtered the livestock.[5] Five years later the French invaded Egypt under Napoleon and brought with them the first modern printing press in Egypt.

Egypt's press may have started with *Al-Ittihad al-Misr* in Alexandria in 1871. Although this newspaper was founded in the latter part of the nineteenth century, it has remained vibrant and occupies offices on Shari Sidi Abd ar-Razzak in Alexandria. With its location on the Mediterranean Sea, the city of Alexandria has always seen lively journalism from newspapers such as *Barad ach-Charikat, Le Journal d'Alexdrie, As-Safeer, Tachydromos-Egyptos,* and *La Reforme.* In Cairo, the newspapers publishing in Arabic are mainly *Al-Ahram, El Shaab, Alalam Alyoum, Al Messa,* and *Al Gomhuria.* Of these, *Al-Ahram* is the largest circulating newspaper. Given the fact that both Cairo and Alexandria are important cosmopolitan centers, Egypt has many foreign language publications including the important English-language *Cairo Times* and the *Middle East Times.*

Egypt is a country with a strong tradition in journalism, although the profession has often come under fire from government officials who are displeased with some of the articles written by the journalists. This tension, between what the politicians see as the need for social and economic development and what the journalists see as the need for democratic development, is at the core of many problems journalists face in Egypt.

The Egyptian journalists have tried hard to maintain their independence in the face of sometimes bitter criticism. They have been criticized by politicians and assaulted by religious fundamentalists for their reporting. Despite the constant threat of harassment and the possibility of censorship, the newspapers in Egypt manage to publish enough news articles that many Egyptians, especially in Cairo and Alexandria, have come to rely more on the newspapers than the television for hard news.

Yet it is true that newspapers must be cautious in countries where the government controls much of what the press does. For example, the government always has in its hands the power to seize the printing presses, to own the newspapers outright, or to control the allocation of newsprint. It takes integrity and a sense of mission for a journalist to suffer abuse from government and still retain a commitment to democratic principles. One of the best examples of Egyptian heroism in journalism is the case of Mustafa and Ali Amin of the popular newspaper *Al-Akbbar.* The publishers were under attack by several governments and created an aura of consistency based on their ill treatment by officials who disliked what they wrote. In fact, Mustafa was arrested twenty-one times in 1950 before the revolution. After the revolution, in 1960, President Gamal Abdel Nasser nationalized *Al-Akbbar* and all of Mustafa's publishing interests. In 1965, Nasser charged him with 165 crimes and imprisoned him. Often in Egypt the aims of *Al-Akbbar* and those of the authoritarian Nasser were at odds; in such cases the journalists almost always lost. In the end, the loss was the people's. In 1974, after being in prison for nearly ten years, Mustafa Amin was freed by President Anwar Sadat. The venerable Egyptian journalist was quoted in the *International*

Herald Tribune (April 8, 1982) as saying: "A free press is a light in the darkness. As far as democracy goes, America had it when its illiteracy rate was as high as Egypt's. If we wait until every Egyptian has a Ph.D. we will never have democracy."

In 2001, the independent newspaper *Al-Nabaa Mamdouh Mahran* published a nonpolitical expose about a Coptic monk who sought favors from the women who visited his monastery. The report was widely criticized by the Coptic establishment and with the urging of Coptic supporters, including some Muslims, the owner of the newspaper, Mahran, and his son Hatem had their membership in the press syndicate revoked. In a powerful statement about freedom of the press, the administrative court rescinded the syndicate's decision that had been based on the claim that Mahran worked in the newspaper that he owned in violation of the rules of the syndicate. Mahran presented evidence that he sold his shares to one of his sons, and Hatem submitted evidence that his wife actually owned his shares.

The case against the Coptic monk was important in that it struck at the protection from scrutiny that many clerics hold dear. What some feared is that the press could seek to expose the sexual lives of the Islamic as well as the Christian clerics. Therefore, the campaign against *Al-Nabaa Mamdouh Mahran* was joined by many groups. Failure to close down the newspaper or to revoke the membership of the publisher and editor meant that Egypt had advanced press liberty one more notch.

Although Egyptian papers have responded to issues of moral turpitude, they have been mostly embedded in discussions of politics. This has been the area in which they have received the most praise as well as the most criticism. This is especially true in regard to the continuing crisis between the Palestinians and Israel. Egypt, having made its peace with Israel during the regimes of Anwar Sadat of Egypt and Menachem Begin of Israel, has a sensitive relationship with Israel. Many incidents and issues complicate this relationship from time to time.

Like television in all capitalist countries, the role of advertising is essential. Egypt has a diverse media that has responded in a truly modern way to the many themes in contemporary life from Al-Qaeda and Osama bin Laden to Milano or Paris fashions, from the Palestinian state to the role of Colin Powell (an African American) in international politics. But the difficulty with the media institutions is that some of them have money and support and others do not. In fact, it is clear that the newspaper giants—*Al-Ahram, Al-Akhbar,* and *Al Gumhuriyya*—are well supported by the state and advertising, while the smaller companies are losing advertising dollars and being marginalized. In fact, the leading opposition newspaper *Al-Wafd* has lost support and its political teeth to the point where it consistently supports the government's positions. Now the main opposition newspaper is *Al-Shaab*, a bi-weekly, however, this paper was suspended by the government after a clash between religious students and the police when the paper ran a campaign against a novel.

While the Egyptian press is very diverse and freedom of the press is generally paid lip service, there are some worrisome trends for the government. One of them is the development of private newspapers that seek to circumvent all of the legal regulations placed on publications. They are licensed abroad and are often printed in the Nasr City tax-free zone outside Cairo.

However, there does not seem to be any credible threat from these privately owned newspapers. The Journalism Syndicate is headed by Ibrahim Nafie, board chairman of the flagship daily *Al-Ahram*. Furthermore, the state-owned newspapers dominate the ranks of the syndicate and have made it difficult for members of privately owned companies to share in the social and financial benefits that come with being a part of the syndicate.

CINEMA

Egypt is a thoroughly modern country in terms of the availability of cinema. One can see very good Egyptian movies as well as films made by foreign companies. Most cities have cinema houses. Alexandria and Cairo have some of the highest numbers of cinemas in all of Africa. Alexandria alone has the Rio, Odiun, Strand, Ryiaito, Royal, Radio, Metro, and Amer, among other smaller movie houses.

Cinema is popular in Egypt and has continued to gain public approval since the heyday of the film, 1940–1960. Most of the films produced during this period emphasized Egypt's Western orientation inasmuch as the film industry was mainly an innovation from Europe. Films of the period celebrated the urban elite and showed Cairo and Alexandria to be cities of the world. Among the films that are regarded as classics in Egyptian cinema are *Ma'bouda al Jamahir (Diva)* and *Shay min al Khauf* which is a film about fear under the reign of Gamal Abdel Nasser. Another film, although more recognized as a play, is *Raya wa Skina* which is based on the true story of the first two women who were officially executed in Egypt.

The cinema houses show mainly Arabic films, but they are also showing increasing numbers of foreign films. What is more unlikely is to locate the best places to see documentary films by some of Egypt's finest filmmakers, although they are finding their way into the international arena. For example, Tahani Rached's 1997 documentary, *Four Women of Egypt*, is a powerful portrayal of religious, social, and educational relationships between different types of women. Shahenda Maklad is a Muslim who lost her husband to a political assassination before she decided to pursue political office herself. She is joined in the movie by Amina Rachid, who was raised in a nonreligious, aristocratic household before embracing socialism and seeking to advance social justice for women and the downtrodden. Wedad Mitry is a devout Christian, a militant nationalist leader and author, who is a mentor to Shahenda Maklad. Then there is Safynaz Kazem, a political journalist and strict Muslim. Given the fact that Egypt is a land of many cultural and political strands, the exploration by Rached of these four women's lives is impressive. However, there are many more stories to be told. The documentary could have examined, for instance, the lives of the black Egyptian women of Aswan vis-à-vis the women of the north. It goes without saying that Egyptian theater, like other sectors of the society, has made the black Egyptians almost invisible. Yet the film *Four Women of Egypt* reveals a lot about the reality behind the Western myth of Egypt. Rached has made two important achievements with this film: on the one hand the film has exposed the contradictory elements of Egyptian life and on the other hand it has shown how it is possible for women from different walks of life to discover coherence and meaning.

CONCLUSION

There is a robust involvement with the media in Egyptian society. Egyptian people sincerely love their newspapers and television. All of the arts of broadcasting and media dissemination have thousands of dedicated workers who are committed to the principles of democratic media. While the media has a long history in Egypt, that is, since 1799 when the French brought the printing press, it also has a checkered history because so many of the past leaders of the country have wanted to dictate what the media should print or broadcast. Many journalists have been victimized by overzealous politicians who have tried to keep critical information from reaching the public. Nevertheless, Egypt continues to have courageous champions of the democratic press and unquestionably they have become the leaders of journalism for many in the Arabic-speaking world. Spurred on by Abu Dhabi and Al-Jazeera, Egypt, with its more than ample intellectual resources for a democratic media, will probably take up its leadership in the broadcasting of hard news from various spots around the world. The lack of a strong investigative reporting cadre is something that has been lamented by the most astute observers of the Egyptian society.

NOTES

1. So when we speak of popular culture, we are doing nothing more than talking about a mode of recognizing what is current in the mass public. Thus, the person

who is able to refer to something that has appeared on television or in a movie is said to be "in," as in "inside" the culture. But this is not to be misunderstood as popular culture in the Western or American sense, but as an awareness of what has occurred in the media.

2. It should also be noted that Information Minister Safwat al Sherif sought to modernize Egyptian visual media in the early part of 2000. He launched the construction of the massive Media Production City (MPC) outside of Cairo and also established two Egyptian satellite channels as well as introduced selected foreign satellite channels. The complex has been declared a "media-free zone" to encourage clients to take part in the MPC. Actually Al-Jazeera, the Qatar satellite channel, has taken up space for producing and broadcasting some programs from the MPC. It is still too early to tell if Al-Jazeera's no-holds-barred, open, and free approach to broadcasting can exist for long as a part of the MPC. Watched by millions of viewers across the Arabic-speaking world, Al-Jazeera has become a forum for debate on human rights, fundamentalism, and corruption. It has offended just about every Arab nation.

3. This may very well be a part of the Arab culture that does not have to bow to Western traditions of the structure of media. Nevertheless, there are enough people in Egypt and perhaps now in other Arabic-speaking nations that object to what has been seen as a ritual tradition in the Arabic culture for this practice to be called into question.

4. See Armbrust (1996, 13). Nevertheless, however one sees it, the catchphrase became a recognizable symbol out of the culture.

5. See Ziegler and Asante (1992, 92).

7

Literature, the Performing Arts, and Music

LITERATURE

MODERN EGYPT, although on the African continent, is a nation overlaid with the Arabic culture and as such it has become the heart of Arab civilization. Egypt has been at the forefront of Arabic literature from the early nineteenth century. In one sense it is possible to speak of the reign of Muhammad Ali as the beginning of the modern tendency in Egyptian literature. During his reign, Egyptian literature expressed a self-conscious awareness of its authentic national development and Egypt was no longer merely the playground of the mighty and the powerful nations and movements that seemed to rule it without reference to the substance of the country's history.

Arabic is the official language of the country although a considerable number of people speak Nubian languages as well as English and French. Language history in Egypt is quite complex. The ancient language was *Mdw Ntr*, (the "Divine Language"), and its script was referred to by the Greeks as hieroglyphics. The Greeks, who arrived in Egypt during and after the ninth century B.C.E. and continued as students in Egypt until the conquest by the Macedonian king Alexander in 333 B.C.E., had a pronounced influence on the language of the Egyptians until the conquest by the Romans when certain Latin expressions became part of the language. Nonetheless, the Greek influence was still prevalent in the language and eventually the Coptic language— a combination of the Greek alphabet and nine ancient Egyptian letters— was formed. Thus, Coptic, as spoken, is the closest language to ancient Egyptian, although it is written in essentially Greek characters. Arabic came in force to Egypt in a campaign led by General El As in 639–641 C.E., and by the ninth century of this era Arabic had dominated the society as the principal language. The last written hieroglyphics, or *Mdw Ntr*, had been carved on the walls of the Temple of Philae around 589 C.E.

Since the Arabization of Egypt the language has become the lingua franca for other Egyptian people, including Copts and Nubians. At various times Greek, Turkish, Russian, French, and English have competed with Arabic in the markets and administrative bureaus of the society. But the advance made by Egyptian writers—particularly Rifa'a Rafi Al-Tahtawi, Yusef Idris, Tawfiq al-Hakim, Taha Hussein (a blind academician of humble birth), and Naguib Mahfouz (who won the 1988 Nobel Prize for Literature)—has been spectacular. They have explored every aspect of the life of the people of Egypt, bringing the modern Egyptian into the arena of contemporary poetry, drama, and fiction. Few Islamic societies have had as rich a talent of writers emerge as Egypt has. They have become familiar with the best literature of the world and as such have added to the international body of literature that could be called modern.

Perhaps no modern society, with the possible exception of France, has such a preoccupation with the purity of language as the Egyptian society does. One finds discussions and articles in the newspapers and magazines about the correct usage of the Arabic language almost everyday. It is assumed that to be a good citizen one must know the difference between sacred and secular language and certainly must not mix the two. One of the most grievous errors an author can make is to misuse the Arabic language—the language of the Qur'an—in popular theater or literature. A host of commentaries attacking the author would normally follow such a misstep. This does not mean that there is no secular use of language in Egypt because there is plenty; it does mean that the users of language must be careful or they will be questioned by the word critics whose responsibility it seems is to make certain that no one crosses the boundary of language. Arabic assumes, for them, the sacred place that it has as the language of the Qur'an and becomes by virtue of its position in the society the only legitimate instrument of "good" expression. This has not prevented Egyptian writers from acquiring secular themes nor has it prevented them from expressing themselves on the evolution and transformation of language itself. A host of humorists and comic writers have appeared with ideas about traffic, crowdedness, housing conditions, the *fellahs* (poor farmers) coming to the big cities, and other aspects of urban living. They are the keepers of the sanity of the masses. But Egypt is not an isolated country, and its writers have not been isolated from the larger concerns of the world; they have expressed their views through fiction as eloquently as any other writers.

MAJOR EGYPTIAN WRITERS

Egypt has produced numerous writers of note. Among the more important are Abdal Rahman al-Jabarti (1754–1825), Rifa'a Rafi al-Tahtawi (1801–1873), Jamal al-Din al-Afghani (1838–1897), Muhammad Abduh (1849–1905), Qasim Amin (1663–1908), Muhammad Husayn Haykal (1888–1965), Taha Hussein (1889–1973), Ali Abdal Raziq (1888–1964), Abbas al-Aqqad (1889–1964), Salama Musa (1887–1958), Tawfiq al-Hakim (1898–), Muhammad Mandir (1907–1965), Louis Awad (1915–), Khalid Muhammad Khalid (1920–), and Naguib Mahfouz (1912–). Indeed, it is Mahfouz, a Nobel Laureate in Literature (1988) and a profound thinker, who has become Egypt's most lucid teller of tales in the contemporary era. He is known best for his strong, simple, direct, and powerful style. Using all of the most precise methods of Arabic, occasionally stretching and flexing the language, Mahfouz is the most popular of the contemporary writers. He has merely built upon the creative traditions of the giants who preceded him.

Most of the writers are especially cognizant of the cultural importance of the Arabic language. They accept a cultural identity in which the proper language is considered extremely important. The *nahda* (renaissance) in culture is dependent on writers recognizing the classical uses of Arabic. In this regard the major Egyptian writers such as Tawfiq al-Hakim in drama, Taha Hussein in autobiography, and Naguib Mahfouz in fiction participated in the *nahda* as modernists who maintain a link to their traditions. They have not given up their appreciation of their Arabic linguistic contributions and have maintained that knowledge of the Western philosophers does not have to destroy one's own sense of cultural integrity.

To give a sense of the Egyptian contribution to world literature, a few of the major figures are highlighted here. These writers represent principal interpretations of Egyptian experiences.

Abdal Rahman al-Jabarti (1754–1825)

The tradition of the scholar and literary personality is long in Egypt, but the presence of the modern writers has thrust the country into the literary leadership of Arabic-speaking nations. No one is any more responsible for starting this trend than Abdal Rahman al-Jabarti. He is one of the three important persons who recorded the French occupation of Egypt (1798–1801). Along with Sheikh Hasan al-Attar and Sheikh Ismail al-Khashab, al-Jabarti might be considered one of the initiators of modernity in Egyptian writing. They may be considered the forerunners of the great Rifa'a Rafi al-Tahtawi. While al-Attar became the leader of the Al-Azhar University and al-Khashab became secretary general of the first Egyptian cabinet formed by the French, al-Jabarti became a cabinet minister in the government of Abdalla Jacques Menou after the 1800 assassination of Jean-Baptiste Kléber.

Al-Jabarti was descended from an Ethiopian—Sheikh Zayn al Din al-Jabarti—who emigrated to Egypt from the Ethiopian city of Jabart around 1600. The family lived in the cloister of Jabartiya in the Azhar compound. Jabarti's great-grandfather became the Mufti of Islam during his lifetime. Jabarti's father—Hasan al-Jabarti—was a cleric and a businessman who owned several houses, a farm, and had three wives and forty children. In 1776, Abdal Rahman al-Jabarti graduated from the Al-Azhar University at the age of twenty-two one year after the death of his father Hasan.

The history of al-Jabarti is that of a man of two worlds. He was certainly of the religious elite, a member of a family that participated in the leadership of Islam, yet he was educated in the highest institution of learning in the Islamic world with access to politics and law. His world was filled with the religious *ulama* and the ruling beys or Mamluks, as well as the Turkish rulers' administration and ruthlessness. None of this seemed to have directed him to writing the *Chronicles*. He was influenced rather by Muhammad Murtada al-Zubeidi, considered the greatest Arabic philologist of the time. Al-Zubeidi had written the famous dictionary *Taj al'arus*. He was a Yemenite scholar who had moved to Cairo in 1754, the year al-Jabarti was born, to teach at Al-Azhar. It was the influence of al-Zubeidi on the young al-Jabarti that caused him to consider writing history. Al-Zubeidi had asked the young man to assist him in writing the biographies of famous men and al-Jabarti diligently applied himself to this task. When al-Zubeidi died, al-Jabarti discovered that he had been commissioned by the Mufti of Damascus to prepare a dictionary of national biography. The dictionary was published but had little impact (Awad 1986, 9).

It was out of this experience that al-Jabarti became intensely interested in chronicles and history. Thus, when Napoleon Bonaparte captured Cairo on July 21, 1798, the forty-four-year-old al-Jabarti was ready to begin the great task of his life. Because he had no Ottoman or Mamluk affinities or loyalties, he served in the French administration of Egypt as a cabinet officer, hoping to bring what he believed were the advantages of Western civilization to his country.

Al-Jabarti found the French legal system superior to that inherited from the Ottomans, and he was impressed by the trial of Suleiman al-Halabi after the assassination of the French leader Kléber. Not only did he find the French system of trials different from the Turkish summary executions, but he was influenced by the way the French dealt with their own soldiers who raped Egyptian women. Of course, because of his deeply religious nature, al-Jabarti could not understand or accept the French liberation of women or the role that women seemed to play in the French civilization. With all of his appreciation of the French legal system and its rationalism, he was still caught in the clutches of his early training. Nevertheless, he did not condemn European civilization but rather praised the French for bringing to Egypt nationalism and a democratic government (ibid., 10).

Al-Jabarti was to find himself in a difficult position when the French were expelled by the Treaty of Amiens in 1801. The charge was laid that he participated with the French, that he collaborated with their administration in Egypt. He soon came out with a self-serving document entitled *Mazhar al taqdis bi dharhab dawlat al-firansis* (Divine Manifestation in the Evacuation of the French). Most writers see this as a diatribe against the French to protect his career (ibid.). After four years of political chaos, during which time the British and Mamluks jockeyed for position and power in the country, Muhammad Ali, an Albanian, finally rose to power in 1805. It was during this time that al-Jabarti started to write the *Chronicles*.

Muhammad Ali punished the *ulama* for resisting his rule, curtailed their privileges in the society, and put some of them in prison. This enraged al-Jabarti, who had finished his work on the French occupation in his *Chronicles*. He then took up the pen against the excesses of Muhammad Ali, calling him a usurper of power in Egypt and not the legitimate claimant to the position of power. He so outraged the Egyptian ruler that al-Jabarti's life was threatened. It was rumored that al-Jabarti was murdered by Muhammad Ali in 1822. However, most authorities believe that al-Jabarti went blind in 1822 and died in 1825, and it was his son Khalil who was assassinated in 1822 (ibid., 11). Although al-Jabarti's writings served as clandestine literature during the time of Muhammad Ali and his successors it was not until Khedive Tewfiq that the ban on his *Chronicles* was lifted. The complete nine volumes of his work were published between 1888 and 1896, with the French translation by Shafiq Mansur Bey, Abdal Aziz Khalil Bey, Nicola Khalil Bey, and Iskandir Ammun Effendi.

Rifa'a Rafi al-Tahtawi (1801–1873)

Rifa'a Rafi al-Tahtawi was the greatest secular nationalist Egyptian writer of his time. Unlike al-Jabarti, Tahtawi was not simply a chronicler of events; he was a political analyst, a critic, and a philosopher of the times. He came from Upper Egypt, the town of Tahta, where he was born on October 15, 1801. After studying as an adolescent, he went to Al-Azhar University to complete his education at the age of sixteen and became the protégé of the scholar and reformer Hasan al-Attar. Al-Attar became the leader of the Al-

Azhar under Muhammad Ali and spent a considerable portion of his time trying to reform the curriculum to include more secular studies to broaden the knowledge of the students.

Al-Tahtawi studied at the Al-Azhar until he was twenty-one years old. He then was an instructor there for two years. In 1824, Ali appointed him to a post as an *imam* in the Egyptian army. When Ali sent some Egyptians to France to gain further knowledge in military, scientific, and technological studies, al-Tahtawi was sent as the *imam* to this group of international students. This was to give al-Tahtawi a major opportunity to improve his French-language skills, to study Western literature, and to learn history, geography, and the humanities.

Muhammad Ali saw the brilliant al-Tahtawi as a possible translator of documents from French into Arabic. The young *imam* studied physics, chemistry, medicine, and mythology while in Paris. His keen mind recorded the political events of the day, including the ferment that led to the overthrow of the monarchy of the Bourbons in the 1830 revolution that brought about the reign of Louis Philippe and the constitutional monarchy in France.

When al-Tahtawi returned to Egypt in 1831, he was received with honor in Alexandria and given land outside of Cairo by Ibrahim Pasha who had heard of his brilliance. In Cairo, Muhammad Ali received him with great joy and courtesy, appointing him to an instructor's post at the School of Medicine. During this time the lectures were given in French and then translated and read out in Arabic for the students. In al-Tahtawi's case he could give lectures either in French or in Arabic. Soon he was made the head of the translation staff because although many of the translators had a good grasp of French, they could not present strong Arabic translations. Since al-Tahtawi had a foundation in Arabic studies at the Al-Azhar and was a skilled *imam*, he could present the Arabic with sharpness and excitement.

Al-Tahtawi's career as a civil servant for the Ali administration brought him many rewards. However, when the cholera epidemic of 1834 hit Cairo, he retired to his Upper Egypt hometown and spent the time translating a French geography book. When the epidemic had run its course, he returned to Cairo and presented Muhammad Ali a copy of the translation. He was made a major in the army and soon became director of the School of Languages. In this school—established as the Madrasa al-Alsun (School of Tongues) in 1835—al-Tahtawi helped to create the foundation for the intellectual *nahda* in Egypt.

The school had a curriculum that consisted of the teaching of Arabic, French, Persian, Turkish, Italian, English, geography, history, literature, and Islamic jurisprudence. The school devoted much time to translating technological documents and lasted for fifteen years. It was closed in 1849 by

Abbas I, the successor to Muhammad Ali. The fanatical and erratic Abbas I closed down all industries started by Muhammad Ali, dismantled the army and the navy, opposed the building of the Suez Canal, and discontinued the only newspaper in the country. He banished al-Tahtawi and his colleague Muhammad Bayumi—a mathematician—to the Sudan. Bayumi could not withstand the strain and died in exile. Al-Tahtawi became the headmaster of a school in Khartoum and spent the time translating French novels.

With the assassination of Abbas I in 1854 and the ascendancy of Said Pasha to the throne of Egypt, al-Tahtawi was recalled to Egypt, promoted, and given high administrative posts. He became the director of the European section in the Governorate of Cairo, then deputy-director and later director of the Military Academy at the Citadel. Yet the greatest achievements of his professional career—the School of Languages and the state-sponsored newspaper *Al waga'i al-Misriya*—were never reopened. His students and followers were relegated to minor posts under Abbas I, and he could never regroup them as he had done at the School of Languages.

Nevertheless, when Khedive Ismail came to the throne in 1863, al-Tahtawi was made the director of the Translation Administration. He was also placed in charge of developing a plan to organize education in Egypt, the seed for the Ministry of Education. Khedive Ismail worked vigorously to modernize Egypt's educational and legal systems and called on the talents of the able al-Tahtawi to lead in the struggle to bring these transformations into existence. Al-Tahtawi went to work right away, calling on many of his former students and colleagues from the School of Languages. The first task was to translate the "Code Napoleon" to be used as the basis of Egyptian law, which laid the foundation for the modern legal system. Thus, al-Tahtawi, the greatest writer and scholar of the times, is responsible for much of the educational system, the legal system, and indeed the modern press in Egypt. Louis Awad makes this observation about the origin of the press in Egypt:

> The first newspaper known in Egypt was the *Courier d'Egypte*, which was published in French by order of Bonaparte to supply the French troops and the local foreigners in Egypt with the important information of the day. Its first issue came out on August 28, 1798, and it lasted for three years, the duration of the French occupation of Egypt. The second periodical was also French, *La Décade égyptienne*, which appeared for the first time by order of Bonaparte on October 1, 1798, and was intended to publish the work of the Institut d'Egypte. With the evacuation these two publications ceased to exist, and the French also took with them the first Arabic printing press. They had brought it to print their proclamations and decrees to the Egyptian people in

the form of posters pasted at street corners and at the entrance to lanes and alleys. The only Arabic book published by the French was the translation of a medical book. (1986, 28–29).

Egypt lived without a printing press for twenty more years until 1824 when Muhammad Ali founded the Bulaq Printing Press. The first newspaper was founded in 1828 under the name *Al Waqa'l al-Misriva*, and was intended to be a government gazette publishing decrees, reports, and achievements. It was bilingual because the official language of Egypt at the time was Turkish. Arabic became the official language—it was already the popular language—in 1873 under a decree of Khedive Ismail. Turkish soon receded into the background, being replaced by French as the second language until the British occupation.

The newspaper had opened under the direction of a Turkish editor who maintained a policy of printing the news in Turkish in the right-hand columns and the Arabic translations in the left. When al-Tahtawi joined the newspaper in 1834, he worked under the direction of the Turkish editor. He was named editor in chief on January 11, 1842. He immediately reversed the former system, placing the material written in Arabic in the right-hand column and the translated Turkish in the left-hand column. No longer were the editorials simply praise songs to the Pasha but analysis and instructive anecdotes. News of Egypt was pushed to the forefront over news from foreign sources, and he soon relegated news from the Ottomans to the second place in the newspaper. Al-Tahtawi introduced literary works into the newspaper to give Egyptian authors an outlet for their creative works. However, "the changes were too revolutionary for the time, and pressure was put on him by the Turkish aristocracy then ruling the country, with the result that Tahtawi had to retreat after one year and most of his brave experimentation and formal changes were rescinded. What remained were the changes in subject matter" (Awad 1986, 29).

Jamal al-Din al-Afghani (1838–1897)

Jamal al-Din al-Afghani's history is uncertain, but his impact on the literary and religious life of modern Egypt is unquestioned. It is believed that he was born in Iran as a Shiite but emerged in Afghanistan as a Sunni activist. In Afghanistan he called himself Jamal al-Din al Rumi (that is the Turk), in Baghdad he called himself Jamal al-Din al-Istanbuli, and in Istanbul and Cairo he went by the name Jamal al-Din al-Afghani. In addition, he bore the title of al-Said, a title used by the descendants of the family of the Prophet Muhammad.

Until he was ten years old, al-Afghani studied Arabic and the Qur'an in his native village under the instruction of his father al-Said Safdar, who was a farmer. He was sent to Qazwin during a feud between local clans; and then when a cholera epidemic broke out in 1850 he was sent to Tehran to finish his studies; and then he surfaced in Najaf, the Shiite center in Iraq where Muhammad Ali is buried. His life there was anything but stable given the political infighting and religious rivalries of the day. In fact, before he was twenty, some time between 1854 and 1857, he had to flee for his life (to India) to escape an assassination attempt by their *Wama* who were fiercely jealous of his "towering genius" (p. 49).

Al-Afghani emerged in Afghanistan after spending time in India and Russia. During the 1860s, a time of instability in Afghanistan, the monarch Dost Mohammad Khan was succeeded to the throne by his son Shir Ali Khan in 1863. He was soon challenged by his half brother Azam Khan. A civil war ensued and Azam Khan was defeated. However, because he was on good terms with the British he was able to find asylum in India. Azam Khan soon argued with the British and resumed his military operations in Afghanistan, capturing the capital, Kabul, in 1866. Part of the country remained in the hands of Shir Ali Khan, and the British refused to recognize Azam Khan's sovereign power. He turned to the Russians for support and soon the name of Jamal al-Din al-Rumi appeared as a counselor to the court. He became a trusted adviser and an intermediary between the Russians and the Afghans for arms and supplies. The British, who had sided with Shir Ali Khan and resupplied his armies and strengthened his defenses, stood to gain influence if Shir Ali Khan was able to retake Kabul. In 1868, his armies, with the British assistance, stormed Kabul and forced Azam Khan into exile in Iran. Jamal al-Din al-Rumi was deported to India—he was barely thirty years old.

A British spy report in 1858 said that al-Afghani was suspected of being a Russian agent and described him as wearing the traditional clothes of the Noghai people of Turkestan, speaking fluent Persian, Arabic, and Turkish. The report prepared by the government in Kabul said that al-Afghani followed the lifestyle of the Europeans more than that of the Muslims. Al-Afghani's liberal conduct created controversy because he refused to observe Ramadan and other Muslim rites. He seemed to enjoy cognac at the Matatia, which was located behind the Opera House in Cairo. In 1879, he was expelled from the Masonic Lodge in Cairo because he publicly denied the existence of God.

During this period, when the Egyptian Nationalist Movement had reached a crucial phase where there was constant agitation and civilian strife, al-Afghani sided with the people who proclaimed "Egypt for the Egyptians." A masterful maneuverer in political situations, al-Afghani managed to place himself on the side of the masses. He gave speeches in Cairo reminding Egyptians of their pharaonic heritage and calling on them to shake the yoke of foreign tyranny and bondage and rise up to assume leadership in their own country. This he did while serving as an adviser and friend to the Tunisian Jew convert to Islam Twetik Pasha, who became prime minister and ruler of Egypt in 1879. His inflammatory rhetoric against political tyranny disturbed the English and Turkish partners in their attempt to keep the Egyptian people subordinated. Al-Afghani's speeches pointed to this Anglo–Turkish policy as antidemocratic. He soon left for Paris where he wrote articles in support of pan-Islam and against the bondage of Islam by Christendom. It seemed that al-Afghani wanted to see an Islam regenerated by modernization. This was his great objective in life, believing as he did that he could use Egypt as a model in the great pan-Islamic experiment.

Taha Hussein (1889–1973)

Taha Hussein is to the twentieth century what Rifa'a al-Tahtawi was to the nineteenth century: the single most important cultural and intellectual influence on the literature of his time. He was born in the province of Minya and became blind at the age of two from ophthalmia. As a young boy he learned the Qur'an and recited it for the benefit of the living and the dead, giving recitations at weddings and at funerals. However, he was more excited by fairy tales than by the Qur'an, according to his autobiography *Al-Ayyam* (1929–1932). This is an important key to his future achievements.

Although he was blind, his father sent him to Al-Azhar University in Cairo in 1902 to complete his studies. He lived with his older brother, who was also a student at Al-Azhar, and went through the usual curriculum of Islamic studies. However, he soon turned to Arabic literature, which had been introduced by the reforms of Sheikh Muhammad Abduh (the religious reformer) and was taught by Sheikh al-Marsafi. Because of his views, considered to be heretical, the young scholar was banned from receiving the *Alimiya* (the degree) until he sat again for his examination. Nevertheless, he studied the classical literature of the Arabic language—still considered a profane subject in Egypt—and mastered the field. He then showed an interest in the secular subjects of modern knowledge such as translated fiction, sociology, philosophy, history, and natural science.

All of this demonstrated that Hussein did not really belong to the Al-Azhar tradition, and in 1910 he transferred to the Egyptian National University, the nucleus of Cairo University. It had been started in 1908 by the Egyptian aristocracy for the promotion of the liberal arts. Its faculty was largely European scholars and a few European-educated Egyptians. By 1914, he had received his Ph.D. for the dissertation on the blind Arab poet and philosopher Ahmad Abdallah al-Ma'arri (973–1057). The dissertation was so provocative that members of the legislature wanted to withdraw the subsidy from the university for producing an atheist like Taha Hussein.

The National University sent him off to France for further study. There he learned French and was a reader at the Sorbonne. He followed courses in Greek, Latin, history, and geography, and received the Doctorat d'Université from the Sorbonne for two dissertations: the major one on the Arab philosopher, historian, and sociologist Ibn Khaldun (1332–1406) and the supplementary one on the basis for the Roman punishment of colonies for disgracing the honor of Rome. In 1919, he was appointed professor of Arabic literature at the Egyptian National University. This was a position he would make great even during his least popular times in Egypt. Having established his position as the greatest figure in Arabic letters during the 1920s—a period when he was the least popular as a writer—he nevertheless maintained his liberal and progressive political positions and loyalties. He explored the tradition of courtly love poetry to prove the apocryphal nature of much of the poetry and to demonstrate that the central figure Qays—the madman of Layla—was a mythical character. This was perhaps "the most controversial and most creative work of critical scholarship for many decades in the history of modern Arabic literature" (Awad 1996, 132).

The masterpiece *Fish-Shi'al-Jahili* (Pre-Islamic Literature), which was published in 1926, for which he was hounded and harassed for many years, caused him great anguish because he knew he had made a major contribution to the understanding of Arabic letters but the established religious figures did not take too kindly to the debunking of some of their most cherished myths. The traditionalists demanded that he be expelled from the university for teaching and writing heresy. His trial before the courts and the suppression of his book—considered blasphemous for daring to question the authenticity of pre-Islamic Arabic literature and having the audacity to call Abraham, Ismail, Hagar, and even the construction of the Kaaba in Mecca within a mythological framework—took a toll on the blind literary giant. Times were difficult. Indeed, "it took no less than Adli Pasha and Zaghlul Pasha to save him. Adli, then Prime Minister, threatened to resign if Taha Hussein were removed or the independence of the University were tampered with. Zaghlul, then President of the Chamber of Deputies, scolded Abd al-Hamid al-Bannan, who had lodged the interpellation against Taha Hussein in Parliament, for interfering in matters he knew nothing about, and caused him to withdraw his charges" (ibid.). Nevertheless the public prosecutor, in order to calm the public, ordered that Taha Hussein's book be withdrawn from circulation.

By the end of the 1920s, Hussein's protectors had passed from the scene and the Crown grew more powerful. He was dismissed from the university, where he had become Dean of the Faculty of Arts. Between 1931 and 1952 he produced little literary work but a lot of political polemics and held numerous positions in the Wafd Party and was reinstated at the university as professor and Dean of the Faculty from 1936 to 1938. But when the Wafdist fell from power, Hussein was mobbed in his office by Fascist students.

In 1938, his famous book *Mustaquabal ath-Thaqafah fi Misr* (The Future of Culture in Egypt) was published. It was a cultural manifesto in which he argued that Egypt was a Mediterranean culture and should remain so. He recommended the teaching of Latin in secondary schools and the study of Roman history. Taha Hussein was once again removed from the position of Dean of the Faculty.

In 1942, the Wafd Party was returned to power and Hussein was again in business to carry out his reforms. Appointed an adviser to Minister of Education Najib al-Hilali Pasha, Hussein launched an intense campaign to secularize all the schools and to add more universities to the system of higher education. He called for the abolition of Qur'anic schools, which he saw as less than liberal educational institutions meant to give the impression that the poor were being educated. In 1943, he founded the University of Alexandria and became a social thorn in the side of the established religious figures. By 1944, he was again on the outside of government and took several positions in literary magazines. He worked with the *Scribe Egyptien*, "an Arabic publishing house owned by a family of Egyptian Jews, the Harari brothers, who published the monthly cultural magazine *Al-Katib al-Misr*, probably the finest cultural magazine Egypt has ever known" (Awad 1996, 134). However when war broke out in Palestine over the creation of the state of Israel, the Egyptian government closed the magazine accusing the owners of being Zionist. These were the worst times for Taha Hussein, a man who had seen good and bad times in his career.

When the Wafd Party again won power in 1950 until the time of the revolution of 1952, Taha Hussein was Minister of Education. He immediately started where he had left off in the reconstruction of Egyptian education. He abolished tuition for secondary schools, established Ayn Shams University, and laid the foundations for Assiut University and Mansura University. He declared that education, like water and air, should be administered free of charge to all mankind, and his enemies seized on this term to describe his educational policies. When Gamal Abdel Nasser came to power, Hussein wanted to continue to serve; however, he was given honorary posts with no power.

While Taha Hussein remains the most important person in Egyptian literature of the twentieth century with his demand for freedom of speech and academic research interest, he is, nevertheless, found in the thick of intellectual and political controversies, some of which clearly showed his bias toward European education and away from African or Eastern ideals. Hussein's great contribution may be that he recognized the twin evils of the tyranny of rulers and the ignorance of the masses and tried desperately to eradicate both.

Tawfiq al-Hakim (1898–)

Tawfiq al-Hakim was born in 1898 and is closely associated with the Azbakiya area. He was sent to Paris to study law from 1924 to 1928. Although he studied law, he never obtained a degree because he was absorbed in drama, novels, painting, music, and sculpture. Thus, when he returned to Cairo he was employed in the government in a legal capacity but not as a lawyer. He worked in the office of legal investigations in the Ministry of Education for a time and then wrote a famous work called *Diary of a Country Prosecutor*—which was published in 1937 in eight languages, including German, French, Russian, Hebrew, and English—recounting his experience working in the legal field as a rural investigator. Between 1939 and 1943 he worked in the Ministry of Social Affairs from which he retired on a small pension to devote his time to his true love: literature. He joined the weekly *Akhbar al-Yawm* in 1945 and worked until 1951 when he was appointed the Director of the National Library. He spent the considerable part of his career with the Higher Council for Arts and Letters and the daily newspaper *Al-Ahram.*

Al-Hakim produced three classic works that created intellectual discussion and controversy but also showed his literary skills as a major force in Egyptian letters: *Al-Yaood* (The Return of the Soul), 1933; *Scheherazade,* 1934; and the play, *Shaab Al-Ulwa* (The People of the Cave), 1934. Taha Hussein was disturbed that Tawfiq al-Hakim had used the vernacular language in dialogue rather than classical Arabic. As a purist, Hussein believed that al-Hakim had created the opportunity for other writers to avoid using the best Arabic in their novels and plays. Yet, Hussein found in al-Hakim elements of genius that came out in the seriousness with which he bridged the gulf between art and religion. Critics who were politically conservative thought that al-Hakim had committed a sacrilege because he drew on religious and sacred texts and subjects to write his novels and plays. In response to the conservative critics, al-Hakim wrote a fundamentalist drama called *Muhammad* in which he demonstrated that one could be an artist and not depart from the religious doctrine.

One has to see that al-Hakim's *Muhammad* is the context of the growth of Fascism as represented by the Young Egypt Party and the development of the Muslim Brotherhood. It was necessary for the artist to at least show that he understood the cultural milieu out of which the criticism came. This was the meaning of al-Hakim's religious writings.

In 1957, President Nasser awarded al-Hakim the second highest decoration in the country: the Grand Collier of the Republic. In fact, only Tawfiq al-Hakim, of all the old guard writers, remained in good standing with the revolutionaries. More influential writers were brushed aside or ignored, but al-Hakim survived and was respected in the regimes of both Nasser and Anwar Sadat.

The Novel

The first modern Egyptian novel appeared in 1914. From that time until the revolution that brought Gamal Abdel Nasser into power, novels were written, but there are perhaps no more than twenty books worth mentioning. Nevertheless, the novel has caught on in Egypt and today there are many prominent Egyptian novelists, including Naguib Mahfouz (1912–) who is a Nobel Laureate in Literature (1988). To gain some appreciation of the achievement of Mahfouz one must remember that he was born in old Cairo, two years before the publication of the first Egyptian novel. He studied philosophy at Cairo University and became a civil servant working for the government in 1939. From this position he could study the insides of the colonial and monarchical bureaucracies of Egypt. In 1954, he joined the Ministry of Culture, finally finding a position that would allow him to make a living and continue writing. Since 1939, Mahfouz has published more than forty novels and many short stories; it might be said of him that he is Egypt's most prolific author and its most characteristic writer. He confronts the depressing situation in the slums of Cairo and paints a picture of hopelessness that usually ends with death. His writing, much like that of the poets who lived a generation later, is gloomy. Yet Mahfouz gathers enough of the soul of Egypt into his novels to present a possibility of victory over depression. Some of his novels have been made into popular Egyptian films.

Another novelist and writer of note is Yusuf Idris (1927–). Idris has also been a prolific writer, penning more than twenty-five volumes of drama, short stories, and novels. He sets his works in contemporary society but has always been more interested in the individuals than the society. He is unlike Mahfouz in this regard. While Mahfouz is wedded to the political, Idris is sure that the person is more important than any political system.

Poetry

Arabic poetry in Egypt harkens back to the days when the Bedouins sang odes to their war heroes. Modern Egyptian poetry has been expressed as romanticism, mysticism, neoclassicism, social realism, symbolism, surrealism, and social revolution. The poets of Egypt have advanced Arabic poetry in tandem with those of the Arabic-speaking world. Finding inspiration in the work of the Syrian poet Adunis (Ahmad Said), many Arabic-speaking poets in Egypt and other places have found their voice in search of a new society. Adunis was committed to a revolutionary vision, and while many Egyptian poets have not been able to commit to revolution, they have committed themselves to nationalism. Adunis' reputation is massive in the Arab-speaking world and has influenced many of the most famous Egyptian poets.

Since poetry is the traditional form of Arab literature, it was not long before Egypt expressed itself uniquely in this area. Among the poets who have encouraged the emergence of a new Egyptian voice in poetry have been Ahmed Shawki, commonly referred to in Egypt as the "prince among poets"; Salah Abdel Sabur (1931–1981), the wise one; Muhammad Al-Faituri (1930–); and Ahmad Hijazi (1935–). All made a fundamental impact on poetry in Egypt; however, the latter three, considered Egypt's greatest poets, directly influenced the style of the poets who followed came after them.

Sabur was educated at Cairo University, where he began to write poetry that expressed social realism. By 1954, he was deeply devoted to questioning the fate of Egypt. In his poem "People in My Country," he lamented that the "people in my country are hawk-like, rapacious." In Sabur's mind, the Egyptians "kill, steal, belch, but they are human, and good hearted when they possess a handful of coins and believe in Fate." His earliest poetry was troubled by his pessimism; however, in his later works, he moved toward a more spiritual and mystical language, seeking, perhaps, a way out of the quagmire of hopelessness and fate. The death of Gamal Abdel Nasser in 1970 struck Sabur as particularly harsh. He wanted to know, "Can he who gave to life die, really die?" Of course, Nasser's death was a big blow to the Egyptians who had found in him a messiah-like figure. Sabur's poetry must be read within the context of his time. He was devoted to the transformation of Egypt and he wanted to see it move vigorously into the modern world.

The poet Muhammad Al-Faituri was of the same generation as Sabur, but he had a much broader vision of Egyptian life. Al-Faituri saw Egypt as African and Arab, as black and white, as ancient and new, and he incorporated in his poetry the image of an Egyptian society in which Africans and Arabs would live side by side as brothers. He was a black Egyptian, one of the few non-Arabs who rose to prominence in poetry during the period of Nasser's golden years. Much like the pan-Africanism that Nasser preached alongside his compatriot Kwame Nkrumah of Ghana, Al-Faituri wrote of Egypt within the ranks of Africa. His collection of poetry bore the titles *Remember me, Africa, Songs of Africa,* and *A Lover from Africa.* He remained a visionary who saw the lives of the black people in Egypt connected to the lives of blacks in other countries.

Another poet who has had a major influence on Egyptian writing is Ahmad Hijazi who was born in a village in Lower Egypt and moved to Cairo for higher education. He was lonely and alienated in the huge city, and his early poetry reflects his dislocation in the urban area. His first collection was called *City without Heart* in reference to the coldness he found in the metropolis. Hijazi's poetry became increasingly tied to the ideology of Socialism during the time of Nasser—he could not break himself away from Arabism, to which he was emotionally tied. However, he found his own community—the one he lacked when he arrived in Cairo—among his political affiliates and became one of the leading poets of Socialist Egypt.

PERFORMING ARTS

Drama

Western-style drama was introduced into modern Egypt because of European influences. Although the short story was the predominant mode of expression in the 1950s (during the time of the Nasserite Revolution), the dramatic play came into its own as the most dominant literary form. It was immediate, dramatic, and political. Theater crowds came to expect that there would be solutions to their problems from the dramatic resolutions.

The Egyptian government has supported the opening of small theaters and has also encouraged the publishing of dramatic texts. This has increased the number of theatergoers and has contributed greatly to a much more conscious theater audience. Of course, the quality of plays also has helped to legitimize the art form.

In addition, one of the great writers of modern Egypt, Tawfiq al-Hakim (1898–), has dominated the stage with his prolific publication of plays, short stories, and novels. He is Egypt's grand old man of letters. Al-Hakim wrote over thirty long plays and many more short plays, which cover a wide range of themes, from philosophy to criticism. He has written on social issues and has even explored the theater of the absurd. In 1959, he wrote the play *Al-Sultan al-ha'ir* (The Perplexed Sultan), translated in English as *The Sultan's Dilemma.* The theme is relevant to contemporary Egypt but is set several centuries earlier. In the play, a sultan discovers by chance that he is still a slave. In order to be freed, he must be put up for auction, sold, and then freed. A widow agrees to purchase him, agreeing to free him if he would spend a night with her. The prime minister suspects the widow of evil intentions and asks the *muezzin* to unlawfully call the dawn prayer at midnight. The sultan sees the trickery and chastises the prime minister. The sultan desires to carry out the bargain with his purchaser. She agrees to release him and he rewards her. The play was viewed by many as a political play attempting to deal with the question of righting the world by force or by upholding principles. Those who have the power are often challenged by not knowing what to do in given situations. They lose sight of the moral nature of law.

Another playwright, Mikhail Roman, was unlike Tawfiq al-Hakim in many ways. For one, he was a scientist who taught at the Institute of Industry. He also died at fifty years of age. He turned to drama near the end of his young life but is still considered one of the great playwrights of his generation because of the strong reactions to his work. He was an angry playwright, and his works evoked strong sentiments for or against his positions. Some believe that Roman's plays produced "verbal fighting" when they were produced. Several of his plays were banned, and theaters expecting a ban from the censors often did not take his texts. (Hopwood 1982, 199).

He wrote twelve plays, but only a few of them were produced. *Al-wafid* (The New Arrival), a one-act play, was produced in 1965 after the censors, during Gamal Abdel Nasser's reign, had permitted it to be seen by a special audience for one night. The new arrival comes to a large hotel in the urban area. The hotel has lots of buttons and button pushers and through various encounters the new arrival loses his sense of security and begins to feel like he is facing a soulless technological institution. His insecurity is greatly increased when he is interrogated, when food is promised and withheld, and when the authorities fail to recognize him unless he produces a train ticket. Without it they will not recognize him. Finally he reaches the point of insanity and begins to shout "I do exist. . . . I can't ever become nonexistent. It's impossible. I exist, I do, I'm here!" (ibid., 150).

Yusef Idris (1927–), a short-story writer, also writes plays. He argued for an Egyptian theater that would grow from the organic soil of Egypt rather than from the European theater. He did not want to see Egyptian writers trying to imitate Europeans. *Al-farafir*, his major play, was produced in 1964. It is a tour de force written to deal with the problems of modern man. He tries to demonstrate that the modern man is a complex mix of personality and character. There is no plot to the play, only encounters. The characters who meet represent different viewpoints and must discuss and deal with various issues. He is brilliant in the dialogue between characters. Thus, Mikhail Roman writes his name in the Egyptian history book as one of the most significant dramatists of the society.

In the same tradition as the eminent Tawfiq al-Hakim, numerous other writers, such as Nomaan Ashour (1918–1987) have attempted to present Egyptian life in a realistic manner. Ashour was born in Dakahlia, Egypt. His grandfather's home had a three-room library of books on all subjects, and the young Nomaan spent his early years reading history, literature, and classical Arabic books. His father was an avid lover of theater and the young Nomaan often accompanied him to the theater in Cairo.

Ashour studied English at the King Fouad University—now University of Cairo. He graduated in 1942 with his first degree. He had been an enthusiastic member of the drama club and had participated in the annual Shakespearean play festival. Because the university had a strong Western orientation in terms of literature, Ashour was influenced by Chekhov, Ibsen, and Bernard Shaw. He believed that the function of art, particularly drama, was to deal with the problems of the society.

One of the best dramatists in modern Egypt's history, Ashour came to his position of eminence by writing about real-life conditions confronted by ordinary people. He was eager to show how family relationships and generational conflicts were impacted by the social and political struggles and ideas in the country. His plays are often seen as tragicomedies because he showed the satirical and ironical situations that were possible in any society where you had the interaction of the old and the new. In 1950, he wrote his first play: *Al-magnet* (The Magnet). In it, he dealt with the obstacles faced by people who had to overcome class distinctions. By 1956, when he wrote the play *Shaab Taabeq Awal* (The People Downstairs), he had perfected the discussion and highlighting of modern realism. In this play, he concentrated more on the condition of the lower class, presenting the Egyptian home as a metaphor of the society. Then in 1958, he wrote *Shaab Taabeq Attani* (The People Upstairs) in which he showed people who could not deal with the reality of their situation but still wanted to look down on others. Ashour then wrote *Film zaai* (Fake Cinema) in 1958 and *Al-Aadel al-Waded* (The Fair Sex) in 1960. They did not receive the same acclaim as his earlier plays. In 1963, he wrote his most famous play *Al-Housh al-Dughry* (The House of Al-Dughry) which portrayed discord and confusion in the Al-Dughry family because of selfishness, greed, and materialism. It became a television serial in the 1980s.

Among the younger dramatists is the prolific Lenin Al-Ramli (1945–), who was born in Cairo. He was not as much a tragicomedian as Ashour, but rather a comedian of sorts. He looked at the daily lives of people and tried to write about the humor he saw in their situations. In some instances this bordered on an examination of the absurdity of certain experiences.

Al-Ramli worked for the Ministry of Culture after he graduated from the High Institute for Theatrical Arts in 1970. In 1983, he resigned from the ministry to devote his full attention to writing plays for the theater. His first play, published in 1972, was *The Word Now is for the Defense*. This was the beginning of a very productive career. Since the early 1970s, Al-Ramli has written more than twenty plays, all of which have been produced, either by public or private theaters. Among his most famous works are: They Kill Donkeys, Don't They?; The Lesson is Over, Stupid; *Ali Bev Mazhar*; Congratulations; Weak Point; Try to Understand Stupid; Lock Up Your Daughters; You're Free; The Scandal; The Uncivilized; Insanity; A Ghost for Every Citizen; *Ahlan; Ya Bakawat; A Point of View;* and *B'il Arabi el Fasih.*

By the turn of the century, there were many young writers and directors trying to move Egyptian drama forward. When Nomaan Ashour tried to Egyptianize foreign texts in the 1960s his efforts were met with some resistance. By the 1990s, the young comic director Nader Salah El-Din had begun to show his flair for theater with the 1995 *Foulan Kaman wi Kaman* (So-and-So Again and Again), a funny spoof of Yusef Chahine's movies. He soon turned his attention to Shakespeare's *Othello,* a play that has received acclaim around the world. El-Din sought to make *Othello* a Nubian doorman, a sort of bumbling, naive stereotype. The audiences found it funny when the actor playing the lead role, Khaled Saleh, refrains "*enta el-habeen ya Daydamoona*" ("you are my darling Desdemona") in a stereotypical accent. There are certainly some funny scenes in this comedic rendering, but it is difficult to get past the fact that Khaled Saleh plays the lead in blackface when there are so many possibilities of black actors, that is, Nubian actors, in Egypt. It borders on distaste much like the old blackface performances in U.S. dramatic productions during the 1930s.

Throughout the 1990s and into the twenty-first century, the actor Karim Abdul Aziz, the son of the famous director Mohamed Abudul Aziz and the nephew of the veteran filmmaker Omar Abdul Aziz, became one of Egypt's new acting stars. He made his film debut at the age of five in the movie *Al Mashbouh* (The Suspect), opposite superstar comedian Adel Imam and versatile actress Souad Hosni. The young actor put on an impressive performance. He worked with the legendary Ahmed Zaki, Layla Olwi, and Sanaa Gameel. Karim has become popular for his role in the television smash-hit *Mar-a Amer al-Jameel* (A Woman from the Age of Love) with actress Samira Ahmed. Every indication is that Karim will continue to be an actor of great versatility. Like other actors in Egypt, Karim has gained much national and international notoriety for his skills. Egyptian actors are the best known in the Arabic-speaking world.

Dance

Dance in Egypt, as in other parts of Africa, plays an important social role in the lives of the people; they dance whenever there is an occasion for celebration. Thus, one would normally find dance performances in the home, at hotels, and at community centers whenever there is a birthday, wedding, or party to commemorate the promotion of a person to a higher office or job. Egyptians love to dance, and they are experts at determining when a person or group of performers is considered good.

There are numerous dances in a country like Egypt, but one of the most visible is the belly dance, which probably came into Egypt with the Turks. Its name in Arabic is *raqs sharqi* (dance of the East); in Turkish the name is *Oryantal* (eastern dance).

In Egypt the role of the female singer and dancer has been an intricate part of the fabric of the society since the nineteenth century. In fact, the *al-jeel* style of belly-dance music is popular music with the youth in Egyptian cities. This style first emerged in the 1980s when the young Egyptians pushed to have music they could dance to. Most of the lyrics are about patriotism. Among the vocalists who sing in this style are Mohammed Moneer, Khedr, Adel El-Musree, Ehab, Amr Diab, and Hanan.

The belly dancer is not merely a dancer but a symbol of style. There are several styles of clothes used by the belly dancer, but the most common is the *bedleh*, a suit of cabaret style. It has beads, a bra, belts, a skirt, and a body stocking and is used for most performances. After performing *raqs sharqi*, the dancer goes backstage and changes costumes. She then comes out in a *beledi* dress to do a folkloric dance. The floor-length *beledi* dress is made of natural fiber such as cotton and is covered with paillettes attached to short fringes of rocaille beads. The belly dancer will also have a cane, an appropriate prop to use when wearing the *beledi* dress and dancing the *raqs al assaya* (the cane dance). The cane dance, which is not just a belly-dance act, is enjoyed by people all across Egypt. It may have derived from Nubian dances in southern Egypt.

Belly dancing is usually accompanied by several instruments, including the dumbek drums. They are normally ceramic with the head of the drum made from either goatskin or fish skin. Many dumbeks now have synthetic heads and the drum body may be made of metal in contemporary Egypt. Another instrument used in the belly-dance performance is the *Kawaia*—a type of Egyptian flute made from a reed that resembles the southern Egyptian *Ney*—

Traditional dancers

sometimes called a *shalabeya*. In fact, this type of flute is very old; it appears in drawings on the walls of the temples. The *rababa* (a stringed instrument), often used in the dance music of the *Saidi* (southern Egyptians), is also used in most Egyptian belly-dancing performances. Other instruments, that may also be used are *sagat* (cymbals), *riqq* (tambourine), *tar* (a large tambourine), and *zurna* (an oboe-type instrument).

There are several other dance styles and types that suggest how important dance is to the Egyptian. One dance is called the *raqs al nashar'ar*. This is a woman's dance that was imported from the Gulf States. The rhythm for the music is called *Saudi*, because so many of the songs come from Saudi Arabia. Examples of this music may be found in the modern hotel clubs in Cairo frequented by many Persian Gulf visitors. The footwork in the dance begins when the dancer steps forward on one foot, brings the ball of the back foot forward, then steps forward again on the same foot. The dancer pauses very briefly and then repeats the whole movement with the other foot. The fundamental movements of this dance are hand movements holding the *thobe al nasha'ar* and head tosses. The *thobe* (Arabic word for dress) is a type of costuming worn to cover the party clothes underneath.

A man's dance, the *Tahtiyb*, is done in southern Egypt. It is a martial arts dance in which the men enact fighting with long sticks as weapons. It is believed that the *raqs al assaya* arose as an imitation of this ancient traditional dance of Nubia.

There is also the *raqs al shamadan* (the wedding dance), a dance that is performed with the dancer wearing a large, ornate candelabrum on her head. The word *shamadan* means candelabrum in Arabic.

Whether the traditional dances of the Saidi or the modern dances of the urban communities such as Cairo, Alexandria, or Hurghada, dance in Egypt remains closely connected to the aspirations of the people. In some areas there are clear distinctions between dances for men and those for women. In the modern cities, men and women can dance together in social dances, but the traditional dances are always ones in which men and women dance in groups. Each traditional dance has some history in place, action, or historical event.

Professional musicians and dancers are found throughout Egypt and anyone can hire them for weddings or parties. Many dancers make their living on the tourist trade. They are contracted to certain tour companies or shipping lines for performances when the large tourist boats are in dock. Many musicians and dancers are under contract to perform four and five times per night, going from boat to boat.

In the end, the best performance is also collective. When a dance performance has been judged outstanding by the audience, it is usually because the dancers, who may also be the musicians, have succeeded in getting the audience to participate in some train of dancers moving around in a circle. The steps of the Egyptian dances are fairly easy to learn and, thus, promote audience participation.

There is no society in which dance is appreciated any more than Egypt. The people have an esprit de corps that is grounded in their love of happiness and joy. Loud shrills, normally made by women, are heard when the music is particularly good and the dancing is very enjoyable. This type of ululation is often associated with highly skilled dancers who are masters of the style and patterns of the most popular music and dance. Thus, Egypt should be seen as a rich cultural environment for traditional and modern dance. New avenues of dance are being discovered and created everyday by the highly mobile and sophisticated youth of the major cities. It is certainly true that most of the vitality in the dance is because of its rich roots, but it is equally a fact that the contemporary customs and culture are built on new dimensions of creativity and power.

MUSIC

The Musical Genius of Abd al-Wahhab

Egypt has produced many musicians but only one of the influence and stature of Abd al-Wahhab. He was considered a genius as a young man and as an old man was venerated by the younger generation for his artistic leadership. But al-Wahhab must be viewed not as a folk artist, though the folk loved him, but as one of the rarefied makers of culture in the Egyptian society. Therefore, he takes his place in the artistic panoply alongside Taha Hussein, Naguib Mahfouz, Tawfiq al-Hakim, and the poet of the elite, Ahmad Shauqi. These are, by any standards, the giants of the artistic world in Egypt.

Abd al-Wahhab was born around the turn of the twentieth century. There has been much speculation as to whether he was born in 1901 or 1910. What is certain is that he died on May 3, 1991, and his death meant that Egypt had lost one of its greatest performers.

The media reacted to Abd al-Wahhab's death with commemorative programs and biographies. They eulogized the great artist as a giant, as one writer said, "with one leg in the East and one in the West, a great tree with its roots sunk deeply into the Arabic musical culture, its branches reaching into the culture of Western music" (Armbrust 1996, 64). While the media lauded praise upon him, the opinion of the regular folk was mixed: some saw him as the keeper of the high culture of Arabic music and others saw him as a panderer to bourgeois tastes. Al-Wahhab suffered from the split vernacular— the double personality—of so many artists in Egypt. He had to maintain Arabic authenticity while simultaneously trying to project modernity. These two tendencies did not have to be contradictory or confrontational, but they often became so in the minds and hands of lesser people.

Abd al-Wahhab loved music from the time he was a young boy. When he was a teenager the story is told that a popular musician passed by in a car. Young al-Wahhab ran after the car and leaped on the running board to get a glimpse of the great singer Salih Abd al-Hayy. He was considered the popular singer of his day. When al-Hayy saw the boy he called for the driver to use the whip on him, whereupon al-Wahhab was knocked off of the running board. He never expressed bitterness about the incident and vowed that he would see his love of music become recognized universally.

Prior to the revolt against the British at the beginning of the twentieth-century, Egyptian culture, particularly in terms of musical talent, was considered crude. It would be Abd al-Wahhab who would rescue the art and become known as the singer of "kings and princes." But all of this would occur after 1920 when Ahmad Shauqi introduced him to high Egyptian society. This did not bring al-Wahhab immediately into the consciousness of the Egyptians; it took some time. He held numerous concerts in numerous venues in order to establish his reputation as a singer. This was made easy by the many weddings and festivals that took place in Cairo.

Some writers have contended that al-Wahhab took Egyptian singing from the level of lewd songs performed before drunken men in tents to the most elegant halls in Cairo. But the authors are careful to craft the rise of the star along traditional lines. Thus, when al-Wahhab reached the highest levels of the art and the widest recognition as an artist, his biographers were eager to show how he simply extended the valued traditions of the society.

There were two traditions that appeared to merge in al-Wahhab's art, that of the folk tradition articulated by the singer Sayyid Darwish and the classical tradition found in the work of the poet Ahmad Shauqi. Because of this combination of the folk and the classical, al-Wahhab was able to maintain a solid audience who understood him as the best in Egyptian singing. He had classical voice training, and his association with Shauqi gave him the authenticity he needed to declare himself above the colloquial expressions of the most naive singers, yet he based his musical lineage in the folk culture of the people. This was a tough feat, but it made him the major singer of the twentieth century. It may be true that al-Wahhab rescued Egyptian singing from the decadence of seedy backrooms where drinking and smoking of hashish was plentiful, but this is not his most important contribution to the history of Egyptian culture.

Egyptian music had found in al-Wahhab a person who could, by his training and experience, reconcile the civilization and heritage of the Arab world with the civilization of the West—this is his most important contribution. Al-Wahhab is best seen as the Egyptian singer who transcended the limitations of his time and place. In fact, he transcended by wrapping himself in his culture and respecting the common person.

An Innovative Composer

Rifaat Garana is one of the most innovative composers in Egypt because he explored the use of the *qanoon* (an instrument used mainly to accompany belly dancing) as a major concert instrument. He spent a lifetime trying to situate Egyptian music as world class. If anyone has done anything to ensure that the music critics appreciate contemporary Egyptian music, it is the brilliant Garana.

He was born around 1925, educated in Egypt by several prominent composers who lived in Egypt during the 1940s, and spent his career advancing Egyptian music. He won the 1966 National Encouragement award, and one year later was given the First Class Order of Arts and Sciences. He chose the concerto form to experiment with the *qanoon* and to represent Islam through the instrument. He played the first movement with the *Eid* prayers; the second with the song "*Talaa El-Badro Alaina*" ("The Moon Rose on Us"), suggesting a link with the prophet's flight from Mecca to Medina; and the third movement was started with the *azaan* (the Islamic call to prayer). In this way, Garana followed history, much like Tchaikovsky symphonically

Musicians playing ancient Egyptian instruments

documented Napoleon Bonaparte's adventures in Russia. His compositions include 23rd of July Symphony, Arabic Symphony, Symphonic Ode to Port Said, Symphonic Ode to the 1956 War, and Symphonic Ode to the Sixth of October.

Music for the Twenty-first Century

Egyptian music has reached international stature by virtue of the country having some of the most accomplished contemporary musicians and the ability of the Egyptian people to improvise groups that enjoy the new music. A group of professional women musicians calling themselves "Banat el Nil" (Daughters of the Nile) held their first concert in 1998. They made an immediate impression on the public because of their talent and professionalism. The group was founded by three women: Dr. Mirvat Garana, Dr. Hanaa Tanious, and Mayyada Salah Eddin. Garana and Tanious had known each other from the time they were four years old. They attended the Higher Music Institute, earned their doctorates, and started teaching the flute and violin—their favorite instruments—at the institute.

The two professors would often ask other women to join them at events to perform for the audiences. When the events were over, the women would go their separate ways. But soon Garana and Tanious decided to put together

Young musician

a group. They selected the name and chose four more musicians to complete the group. They include both Arabic and popular music in their repertoire. They played at the Women's Conference and were asked to play at the closing ceremony for the International Squash Tournament in Hurghada. The group concentrates on the work of Farid El Atrash, Abd al-Wahhab, and Mohammed El Mougi.

A New Diva Is Born

Mohammed Ali Soliman was a singer of some repute, and he started his daughter Angham's instruction in classical Arabic music at age five. She was born in 1975. She did not want to learn science or math; she only wanted to sing. She became like a recorder for her father who would call upon her if he forgot a part of a classical piece. Attending the Higher Institute for Arabic Music, she excelled, graduating in 1993.

At the age of seventeen, Angham became a professional singer with the endorsement of the Egyptian Radio Committee, an endorsement that meant she had passed the test to become an official singer of classical music. The song she performed for the Radio Committee was the classic "*El Gaanna That A'adaamik*" (Heaven Is Beneath Your Feet). This is a song dedicated to motherhood. She was so effective that the Committee immediately asked her to record the song and commissioned a live performance by her for the Mother's Day celebrations.

Since Angham came from a family of musicians, it might seem that she was destined to be a great musician, but she demonstrated unusual commitment to practice and discipline. Thus, her talent might have come from heredity, but her success was due to hard work and study. Her father, uncle, mother, and maternal aunt were all singers. Indeed her paternal grandfather was also a famous musician. Angham is now seen as one of Egypt's greatest divas.

In addition to the women in popular music, there are women who are claiming territory in the classical Arabic musical vernacular. None has experienced the dramatic evolution of her career as has Angham. She sang the classic *"Ashwaq"* ("Longing") when she was five years old without making a mistake. Those who heard the young Angham knew that they had witnessed the budding of a musical genius. It is said that as a child she was either singing or listening to music every minute of her day.

Glossary

Ahwa coffee

Al-bahr gateway to the sea

Alimiya university degree

Ansar helper

Ashaa dinner

Azaan Islamic call to prayer

Baklava layered pastry filled with nuts and honey-lemon syrup

Bedledi clothing worn by belly dancer

Bismillah In the name of Allah

Caliph a successor of the Prophet Muhammad

Chai tea

Dajaaja chicken

Deen religion

Dhikrs Sufi meetings

Ejje omelette

Falafel deep-fried patty filled with spiced ground chickpeas

Farah wedding

Fata a mixture of meat, bread, rice, and vinegar

Fatwa opinion (authoritative verdict) by a canon lawyer

Fellah peasant farmer

Felucca sailboat

Foul   slow-cooked mash of brown fara beans and red lentils

Ful-medames   baked beans

Futoor   breakfast

Galabea   long-sleeved one-piece dress for men

Gebna beida   soft white cheese

Hadith   specific stories or activities of the Prophet Muhammad and his followers

Hajj   pilgrimage

Halawa   sweet sesame cake

Hegira   migration of the prophet to Medina in 622

Hijab   head covering for women

Hummus   dip made from pureed chickpeas

Iftar   large meal eaten after sunset

Imam   mosque leader

Infitah   open-door economic policy

Jihad   Holy War, spiritual quest or military conquest

Karkaday   popular drink made from the hibiscus plant

Kebab   skewered meat cooked over charcoal

Khamsin   hot, fierce, dry windstorm

Khazaan   dam

Khedive   viceroy—title of ruler of Egypt under the Ottoman Sultan, 1867–1914

Mahdi   infallible ruler

Majalla   magazine

Mamluk   a member of the Egyptian military class that occupied the sultanace from 1250 to 1517

Mastaba   rectangularly shaped box

Mawlid   birthday of a Sufi saint

Milabbis   sugar-coated almonds

Misr   Arabic for Egypt

Molokhiya   spinach-like vegetable

Muezzin   a Muslim crier; one who calls Muslims to prayer

Muhajirun   emigrant

Nahda   renaissance

Pastorami   cured beef

Pita   flat, unleavened bread

Qanoon   instrument used to accompany belly dancing

Qur'an   sacred text of Islam

Quraysh   North Arabian ethnic group, Prophet Muhammad's people

Raqs sharqi   belly dance

Rukkab   ordinary; U.S. equivalent is local train

Sabaah   morning

Sahara   desert

Sajaada   carpet

Sakia   waterwheel

Salat el-gomaa   Friday noon prayer

Sayeda   lady

Shaab   people

Shaduf   counterpoise lift

Shahada   Islamic pillar, proclaiming that Allah is the only God

Shammy   flat, unleavened bread

Sharbat   drink made from diluted syrup

Shari'a   Muslim law

Shi'a   Partisans of Ali

Shiite   Muslim believer in Ali's succession to Muhammad

Sufi   Islamic mystic

Sunna   literally, habits; a group of religious teachings

Sunni Muslim   believer in customary succession

Sura   chapter of the Qur'an

Tagen   clay pot

Tahina   lemon and garlic served with a dip

Tariqas   paths; another name for *sufi* orders

Ulama   Islamic scholar

Um al-dunya   "Mother of the World"

Umma   Muslim community of believers

Usra   family

Wafd Party   political party that grew from a 1918 delegation to England

Zaghruta   celebratory wailings of women at a wedding

Zakat   charity or the giving of alms

Zibib   local alcoholic beverage

Bibliography

Abu-Lughod, Ibrahim. *Arab Rediscovery of Europe*. Princeton, NJ: Princeton University Press, 1963.

Abu-Lughod, Janet. *Cairo: 1001 Years of the City Victorious*. Princeton, NJ: Princeton University Press, 1971.

Abdel-khalek, Gouda, and Robert Tignor. *The Political Economy of Income Distribution in Egypt*. New York: Holmes and Meier, 1982.

Ahmed, Leila. *Women and Gender in Islam: Historical Roots of a Modern Debate*. New Haven: Yale University Press, 1992.

Amin, Galal. *Whatever Happened to the Egyptians?* Cairo: American University of Cairo, 1995.

Amin, Qasim. *The Liberation of Women and The New Woman: Two Documents in the History of Egyptian Feminism*. Cairo: American University Press, 2000.

Ammar, H. *Growing Up in an Egyptian Village*. New York: Grove Press, 1954.

Armbrust, Walter. *Mass Culture and Modernism in Egypt*. Cambridge: Cambridge University Press, 1996.

Atiya, Nayra. *Khul-Khaal: Five Egyptian Women Tell Their Stories*. Cairo: American University in Cairo Press, 1984.

Awad, Louis. "Maulahazat ala al-nay wa-al-gamin." *Al-Ahram*, 19 December 1969, p. 6.

Awad, Louis. *The Literature of Ideas of Egypt*. Atlanta, GA: Scholar's Press, 1986.

Ayubi, N. N. *Bureaucracy and Politics in Contemporary Egypt*. London: Ithaca Press, 1980.

Baker, R. W. *Egypt's Uncertain Revolution under Nasser and Sadat*. Cambridge, MA: Harvard University Press, 1978.

Barton, Frank. *The Press in Africa*. London: Macmillan, 1979.

Brooks, Geraldine. *Nine Parts of Desire: The Hidden World of Islamic Women.* New York: Anchor Books, 1995.

Brown, Nathan. *Peasant Politics in Egypt.* New Haven, CT: Yale University Press, 1990.

Burns, W. J. *Economic Aid and American Policy toward Egypt.* Albany: State University of New York Press, 1985.

Butler, Alfred. *The Arab Invasion of Egypt and the Last 30 Years of the Roman Dominion.* Oxford: Oxford University Press, 1902.

———. *The Arab Invasion of Egypt.* Brooklyn, NY: A and B Books, 1922.

Chennels, E. *An Egyptian Princess by Her English Governess.* London: 1893.

Cooper, Mark N. *The Transformation of Egypt.* London: Croom Helm, 1982.

Crecelius, Daniel. *The Roots of Modern Egypt: A Study of the Regimes of Ali Bey al Kabir and Muhammad Bey Abu al-Dhahab, 1760–1775.* Minneapolis, MN: Bibliotheca Islamica, 1981.

Creswell, K.A.C. *Early Muslim Architecture. 2 Vols.* London: Penguin, 1958.

Dessouki, Ali Hillal, ed. *Democracy in Egypt.* Cairo: American University in Cairo Press, 1978.

Diop, Cheikh Anta. *Civilization or Barbarism: An Authentic Anthropology.* Trans. Yaa Lengi Mecmi Ngemi. New York: Lawrence Hill, 1991.

El-Dakhakhni, Mamdouh. *Egypt* (August 2001).

El-Hakim. *Nubian Architecture: The Egyptian Vernacular Experience.* Cairo Palm Press, 1999.

Fahmi, Ismail. *Negotiating for Peace in the Middle East.* London: Croom Helm, 1983.

Faksh, Mahmud. "The Consequences of the Introduction and Spread of Modern Education: Education and National Integration in Egypt." In *Modern Egypt: Studies in Politics and Society,* edited by Elie Kedourie and Sylvia G. Haim. London: Frank Cass, 1980.

Ferneat, Elizabeth Warnock. *In Search of Islamic Feminism: One Woman's Global Journey.* New York: Doubleday, 1998.

Gardiner, A. H. *Egypt of the Pharaohs.* Oxford: Oxford University Press, 1974.

Gharib, Samir. *A Hundred Years of Fine Arts in Egypt.* Cairo: Prism, 1998.

Gibb, Sir H.A.R. *Studies on the Civilization of Islam.* London: Routledge and Kegan Paul, 1962.

Gilsenan, Michael. *Recognizing Islam: Religion and Society in the Modern Arab World.* New York: Pantheon, 1982.

Gole, Nilufer. *The Forbidden Modern: Civilization and Veiling.* Ann Arbor: University of Michigan Press, 1994.

Gran, Peter. *Islamic Roots of Capitalism, 1769–1840.* Austin: University of Texas Press, 1979.

von Grunebaum, Gustave. *Medieval Islam.* Chicago: University of Chicago Press, 1946.

Hansen, Bent, and Samir Radwan. *Employment Opportunities and Equity in Egypt.* Geneva: International Labour Office, 1982.

Harris, Lillian Craig, ed. *Egypt: Internal Challenges and Regional Stability*. London: Routledge and Kegan Paul, 1988.

Heikal, Mohamed. *Autumn of Fury: The Assassination of Sadat*. Cambridge: Cambridge University Press, 1985.

Heyworth-Dunne, James. *An Introduction to the History of Education in Modern Egypt*. London: Luzac, 1939.

Hopwood, Derk. *Egypt: Politics and Society, 1945–1981*. London: Allen and Unwin, 1982.

Hourani, Albert. *Arabic Thought in the Liberal Age, 1798–1939*. Cambridge: Cambridge University Press, 1983.

Hussein, Taha. *The Future of Culture in Egypt*. Washington, DC: American Council of Learned Societies, 1954.

al-Jabarti, Abdal Rahman. *Al-Jabarti's Chronicle of the First Seven Months of the French Occupation of Egypt, Muharram-Rajab 1213* (15 June–December 1798). Leiden: Brill, 1975.

Kamel, Mohammed Ibrahim. *The Camp David Accords: A Testimony*. London: Routledge and Kegan Paul, 1986.

Kedourie, Elie, and Sylvia G. Haim. *Modern Egypt: Studies in Politics and Society*. London: Frank Cass, 1980.

Kelley, Allen C., Atep M. Khalifa, and M. Nabil El-Khorazaty. *Population and Development in Rural Egypt*. Durham, NC: Duke University Press, 1982.

Kepel, Gilles. *The Prophet and Pharaoh: Muslim Extremism in Egypt*. London: Al Saqi, 1985.

Khalidi, Tarif. *Arabic Historical Thought in the Classical Period*. Cambridge: Cambridge University Press, 1994.

Landau, Jacob. *Studies in the Arab Theatre and Cinema*. Philadelphia: University of Pennsylvania Press, 1958.

Lane, Edward. *An Account of the Manners and Customs of the Modern Egyptians*. London: Charles Knight, 1835.

Leo Africanus (al-Hassan ibn Muhammad al-Wazzan al-Fasi). *History and Description of Africa*. London: Hakluyt Society, 1896.

Mabro, Robert. *The Egyptian Economy, 1952–1972*. Oxford: Clarendon Press, 1974.

McDermott, Anthony. *Egypt after Nasser*. London: Croom Helm, 1987.

Mitchell, Timothy. *Colonizing Egypt*. Berkeley and Los Angeles: University of California Press, 1991.

Nelson, Kristina. *The Art of Reciting the Qur'an*. Austin: University of Texas Press, 1985.

Nyrop, Richard F., ed. *Egypt: A Country Study*. Washington, DC: American University and U.S. Government Printing Office, 1983.

Pedersen, Johannes. *The Arabic Book*. Princeton, NJ: Princeton University Press, 1984.

Rugh, Andreas B. *Family in Contemporary Egypt*. Cairo: American University in Cairo Press, 1985.

Said, Edward. *Orientalism.* New York: Pantheon, 1978.

Scholch, Alexander. *Egypt for the Egyptians: The Socio-Political Crisis in Egypt 1878–1882.* London: Ithaca, 1981.

Stewart, Desmond. *Great Cairo: Mother of the World.* Cairo: American University in Cairo Press, 1996.

Tucker, Judith E. *Women in Nineteenth-Century Egypt.* Cambridge: Cambridge University Press, 1985.

Vatikiotis, P. J. *The Modern History of Egypt.* New York: Praeger, 1969.

———. *The History of Egypt.* 3rd ed. Baltimore, MD: Johns Hopkins University Press, 1986.

Waterbury, John. *The Egypt of Nasser and Sadat: The Political Economy of Two Regimes.* Princeton, NJ: Princeton University Press, 1983.

Ziegler, Dhyana, and Molefi Kete Asante. *Thunder and Silence: The Mass Media in Africa.* Trenton, NJ: Africa World Press, 1992.

Index

About the Author

MOLEFI KETE ASANTE is a Professor in the Department of African American Studies at Temple University. He is the author of more than 50 books, including *The Egyptian Philosophers* (2000).